# Aging Is a Family Affair

## How to Prepare for Tomorrow's Difficult Caregiving Decisions— Today

MARY ANN MASSEY, ED.D.

*A Crossroad Book*
The Crossroad Publishing Company
New York

The Crossroad Publishing Company
www.CrossroadPublishing.com

In continuation of our 200-year tradition of independent publishing, The Crossroad Publishing Company proudly offers a variety of books with strong, original voices and diverse perspectives. The viewpoints expressed in our books are not necessarily those of The Crossroad Publishing Company, any of its imprints or of its employees. No claims are made or responsibility assumed for any health or other benefit.

Printed in the United States of America.

The text of this book is set in [Apollo & Helvetica Neue]

Project Management by
The Crossroad Publishing Company
John Jones

For this edition numerous people have shared their talents and ideas, and we gratefully acknowledge Mary Ann Massey, who has been most gracious during the course of our cooperation. We thank especially:

Cover design: George Foster       Text design: Web Fusion
Proofreading: Sylke Jackson       Printing: Versa Press

Message development, text development, package, and market positioning by
The Crossroad Publishing Company

Cataloging-in-Publication Data is available from the Library of Congress

Books published by The Crossroad Publishing Company may be purchased at special quantity discount rates for classes and institutional use. For information, please e-mail info@CrossroadPublishing.com. To learn more about the author, please visit www.AgingIsAFamilyAffair.com.

ISBN 13: 978-0-8245-26238

1 2 3 4 5 6 7 8 9 10          14 13 12 11

# Table of Contents

# Dedication

– Offered in loving memory of Marie and Fred Beyer –

Their deaths gave life to this book.

# Acknowledgments

Talking with people about their feelings and their needs, along with their hopes and their fears, comes easy to me. Writing about the people who have wrestled with their most personal relationships has proven more challenging. I called upon family and friends to read my early compilations, and then I asked for their candid feedback.

Cheryl Sansone and Joan McMahon, both grammar experts, painstakingly edited my sentence structure and paragraph placement in the early chapters. I learned that writers are different from public speakers, and that the repetition necessary for the spoken word is distracting to the reader in the written version. Suzanne Massey, my daughter, and Mary Oles, a good friend, read the manuscript twice (!) for an overall flow of thoughts and the connection of the individual stories to the development of my themes. They both saw the large picture and supported the progress. Paul Sontrop, a long-time Canadian friend, invited me to apply the drama that has defined my public speaking to the written text. Al Ptasznik, my husband and champion, read and re-read edited sections. He has a talent for helping to shape a story's development. He also created private space for me to 'do my thing'. Last among the early readers was a trusted therapy colleague, Dr. Jules Auger, a Lutheran minister centered on his own spiritual walk. He reminded me to hold sacred all aspects of life, including the end of life as we know it. Jules encouraged me not to be afraid to speak on a spiritual level about life's entire journey. I will be ever grateful to him for encouraging me to be myself and to allow others to find their echoes in the various stories I would share, including my own.

Of enormous importance to the evolution of this work into the final product is Sofi Starnes. In my search for an editor, her name surfaced over lunch with a friend. An hour later, I bumped into her in the grocery store. We knew instantly that we would work well together. She has been my inspiration, my greatest cheerleader, and my instructor. Sofi heard my intentions, as I hear those of my clients, on that meta-, below-the-surface level. I have felt loved, understood, and appreciated by her every step of the way. This book became our project; I am thrilled to share the fruits of these efforts with her. Her generosity of spirit and time, as well as her special editorial talent, have been precious to me.

Dr. John Jones, the editorial director for Crossroad Publishing, took what Sofi and I fine-tuned and polished the book. He has brought enlightenment to obtuse paragraphs, and, with intriguing questions, allowed me to strengthen good thoughts. It has been my honor to work with him. His interest, energy, and appreciation of my style and content will stay with me forever.

Lastly, but most of all, I offer my sincere thanks to those who have shared their stories with me. Some I met in passing, some are special friends; in every case, I have been honored to walk with them through difficult even painful times in their lives. They know how much I cherish their journeys. I am grateful for their willingness to let me share portions of their stories. I have changed their names, their specific conflicts, and their places of residence, but I have retained the essence of their experiences. Truth speaks volumes to those of us who see them as pioneers.

# Prelude
## *The Stories We All Face*

During the fall of 2004, my mother was undergoing her second bout of cancer. I was nearing sixty. My siblings and I were very attached to her—she had always been our rock—and we were painfully aware that death might take her from us. Rarely did we talk with each other about losing her. Each of us hoped against hope that she would beat the beast again.

We didn't know that we didn't know how to handle what lay ahead. Mom's illness, which had lasted over four years, with two years of excruciating chemotherapy, was the hardest phenomenon we had ever endured as a family. Some of what came to pass we handled well, and other things were so far out of our range of experience that our decisions were guided by ignorance and guesswork.

Then everything changed on January 11, 2005. Mom didn't die of cancer but of something utterly unexpected. As a result, dad's life changed dramatically. Dad, who had always been healthy, would require intensive care, surgeries, and living arrangements that rendered earlier reflections on his future irrelevant. His situation affected us all and threw a wrench into the lives of our individual families.

In a heartbeat, mom's death and the unforeseen horror for dad became a family affair. Prior to these events, I had been vaguely attuned to the changing circumstances that the elderly experience. Hearing loss, forgetfulness, slowness of gait and response, a tendency to repeat stories—these were easy to discuss in the abstract, but they were not the reality I lived with every day. I didn't know that our family would

1

suddenly face the challenge of these changes in our own parent. We, too, would experience annoyance, impatience, and frustration when our instinct was to jump in to help rather than honor the necessarily slower pace of our father. Were we really being helpful or simply managing our own intolerance? The answers were not always obvious. Our lessons were not easily learned.

My parents had started to slow down and deal with physical breakdowns in their late 70s. Bottles of pills lined their cabinets, they took daily naps, and mom, at least, repeated herself often. At that time, really for the first time, I started noticing how other families respected (or didn't respect) their elders. I watched adult children make faces, roll eyes, and grit teeth when a parent walked too slowly, asked "what did you say?" a few too many times, or seemed demanding when seeking help. Of course, the parents knew their behaviors were disturbing their children, but there was nothing they could do about that. Life was physically harder for them than it had been in their younger years.

Because the number of families with aging members has grown exponentially in recent years and will continue to do so, more of us are tuning in earlier to our elders' needs. Stories started drifting my way, even when I was not looking for them. I heard numerous anecdotes about people's struggle to deal with an aging parent, from colleagues, clients, and even cashiers and store clerks. On the phone or over tea, my friends anguished aloud over the *right thing to do* in their family.

In some cases, longstanding unresolved problems compounded the stress and disharmony among them in later years. A surprisingly large number of families, even ones who were otherwise healthy, seemed to be communication challenged. The natural path of growing old in America seemed anything but natural in a great many homes.

Throughout this time, I sensed a need to document every story I heard. I felt compelled to take notes on whatever blank paper I had handy at the time. I registered people's irritations, fears, and fatigue, and I eagerly recorded success stories of renewed family relationships during the aging years. How did the people I met forge a trail through their own private uncharted territory?

On the pages of this book, I share these stories—my own and others' experiences with aging family members— along with some clinical suggestions for gracefully and respectfully creating time to talk with each other. The stories focus primarily on conversations between parents and their children about shifting needs, deciphering the many options for long-term care, and everyone's varying ability to help.

Since my expertise focuses on family communications, my emphasis here is on the conversations between family members. Over many years, I have learned never to underestimate the value and usefulness of talking with each other, even when addressing awkward topics. Silence is deadly and perpetuates frustration. It encourages mind-reading, judging, and other negative and unproductive habits. Alternatively, openness lets grace guide the truth wherever it may lead. Allowing differences of opinion often signals productive exchanges. All conversations are beneficial: for ourselves, for the ones with whom we are sharing the goodbye time, and for our children who will come after us. Whether talking about the early changes or the end changes, communication remains critical to success.

The stories in this book approach aging from diverse perspectives. Some describe family situations in which parents made plans for the future when they were healthy and independent. These stories are easier to discuss because they are not guided by the urgency of illness. Others expose end-of-life fears, struggles, and tiredness. They encourage us to articulate our personal meaning of life and death.

Each section begins with an element of my own family story, followed by a series of stories from other families. The sections also include points to ponder on the healthy processes and choices families make regarding aging parental care, as opposed to some less-than-wise decisions reached unilaterally. These points are largely drawn from my own ongoing studies and weekly clinical experience where clients share their deepest concerns, feelings, and choices in the privacy of my office. Over my thirty-four years as a therapist, there is little that I have not heard.

The narratives are primarily from the perspective of a son or daughter trying to talk to a parent about present or future needs, although some conversations were initiated by a parent attempting to engage a reluctant offspring. Such situations occur whether or not inheritances are at stake. The discussions are not about money or "who gets what." They are about people who struggle to be real with each other during emotional times, on topics of change that are profound and often heartbreaking for everyone.

This book is for those of us who wish to improve family communications. What better way to begin than to listen to some personal stories, where our own dilemmas are mirrored in other people's lives, their choices shedding light on our own? Of one thing we can be certain: life-changing situations await us all during the next phase of this journey. My hope is that the stories in this book will help your family begin your own discussions on the difficult topic of aging.

# 1

## Family Speak

### *The Case for Talking with Aging Loved Ones Sooner Rather than Later*

In 2005, Marie and Fred were driving home from a doctor's visit. It was a beautiful winter day, and all was right with the world. An instant later, their car was hit head-on by a speeding vehicle from the opposite direction. Marie, 83, was killed instantly. Fred, 82, was seriously injured and would never return home.

Marie and Fred were my parents.

With the crash, our family changed forever. Our once independent parents were stripped of the life they knew, and we were forced to deal with death and the maze of professional care. We were ill-prepared for the events that followed. Between visits to dad, in intensive care an hour's drive away, we gathered the family from all parts of the country and conducted mom's funeral.

Like many families who have been in our situation, my siblings, our families, and I went into crisis-resolution mode. We waited for dad to recover, knowing in our hearts that even if he lived, he would probably never walk on his own again. For the better part of a month, we took turns sitting by his side, waiting for infections to heal, learning about titanium hip implants, and signing off on antidepressants and other new medications. While dad's state of shock and fragility masked his own grief, nothing masked ours.

The journey from mom's death to dad's funeral some nineteen months later felt like a course in managing the ins and outs of professional care. Our abilities to think rationally about the best care for dad, based on *his* desires rather than *our conflicting desires for him*, were tested regularly. In the ten years before his death, some of my siblings and I had met only at family gatherings. On those occasions, our conversations were light, filled with holiday spirit or summer fun activities. We had rarely discussed serious personal issues, let alone later-in-life choices for our parents.

The car crash changed all of that. Life invited us to form new relationships with each other. The professional care aspect was unfamiliar and confusing. The co-executors, brothers Jim and John, wanted us all to have a voice. Yet the options before us were complex. Some of us had little to offer at first, leading the quicker thinkers among us to jump in with their conclusions. To those still pondering, the others' suggestions sounded like pronouncements. A degree of small group triangling and covert discussion ensued.

Few of us are at our best in such situations. Members of my family lived far from each other, which meant that we tended to interpret comments or actions without really knowing what the other person intended. There was the usual mind-reading and judging of each other's choices and level of involvement in the process.

## Respecting Differences

Our own family evolution resembled stories I hear from many of my clients, colleagues, and friends. Coming to respect each other's abilities is hard work and takes time to achieve.

If a common experience among families is the natural aging process or age-related illness of a family member, a common challenge is communication. I have labeled the process of communication in this context *Family Speak*— how we talk with each other. The term includes a range of communication successes and blunders. It encompasses not only wholesome but also dysfunctional family styles with rigid rules and unspoken demands, defined by individual self-interests, misunderstandings, and hurt feelings.

When we accept that we are no better or worse than other family members—just different—healthy Family Speak can help us change rooted, hurtful styles and break longstanding impossible rules to accept each person with his or her uniqueness. Healthy Family Speak, meaning open, clear communication and respect for other family members' differences, can and should be a goal for all families even in relatively peaceful times. It strengthens trust and deepens bonds. Then, in crisis times, families can work toward *productive* Family Speak, so vital for dealing with significant family changes.

Productive Family Speak is important for any crisis, but when a crisis involves the major illness of a parent, existing family structures and personal daily activities often shift to include increased care for that parent. The care itself must be wedged in between responsibilities and schedules that are already demanding. Then there are the visits to the parent in need, as well as phone calls to family members about each other's phone calls. Emotions rise. Tensions mount. Dealing with the compounded crisis is overwhelming, no matter how many family members offer to help out with the caregiving responsibilities. The immediate and sometimes all-consuming care for our elders can come to dominate a family.

## Five Factors

My own family's early Family Speak successes emerged through our ability to overcome five significant sibling differences. These same factors are important in any family's success, and we will see them at work in the stories throughout this book.

1. First, we addressed our *different personalities*. Each of us had deeply-rooted styles for how we tended to deal with change of any kind, and this brought about inevitable friction: some made decisions quickly, others had few opinions up front, and still others wanted to wait for dad to formulate his own decisions.

2. We then faced the next challenge: *individual inclinations and choices* relating to this specific set of challenges. These grew out of life experiences and natural preferences. Inevitably, six competing sets of specific wishes—"this is the way we should do it"—would get tangled up at times.

3. These inclinations also fed our *unique personal relationships* with our father. Of course, those of us who shared special interests with dad formed closer, easier relationships with him. The guys talked sports and watched golf and college basketball together. My sister, Jeanne, and I had to become more creative in the ways we connected to him. Jeanne fed him, and we both shared fun family anecdotes, which he enjoyed.

4. Our *physical proximity* to dad was instrumental in deciding how to delegate tasks. Jim, John, and Jeanne live in New Jersey; two other brothers, Bill

and Fred, live in California, while I live in Virginia. Those of us at a distance visited irregularly while the local siblings carried a larger burden, regardless of how close they were with dad.

5. Lastly, we all had *specialized gifts*. Some of us were limited as caregivers but great at dealing with money, for example. So, a selection process emerged for caregiving, managing finances, working with attorneys, organizing data, keeping insurance records, talking on the phone, visiting, dealing with personal feelings about aging and illness, and other such matters. We each found our role, and this helped us develop greater respect for one another.

These five important factors—inborn personality styles, personal inclinations, shared interests with a parent, physical proximity, and specialized talents—should not be minimized. Families succeed when they identify them and take them into consideration when seeking to resolve sibling issues and delegate well. Ultimately, our struggles to communicate clearly and then negotiate our way to some consensus strengthened us and brought us closer during the two weeks after mom's death, while dad was fighting for his life. We came to understand a little better how others managed their own inner worlds, and most of the time, we dealt with our differences respectfully.

When the reflective introverts had a chance to organize and share their thoughts, and the brainstorming extroverts settled down enough to listen, we pushed aside lingering reservations and got down to business. Each serious conversation brought up yet another awkward topic. Would we have an open or a closed coffin for mom? Would she want to be cremated or buried in a casket? Where would dad live?

Who would assume primary care status for him? Encouraged by early successes, we evaluated each other's particular strengths and limitations for succeeding tasks. We learned to listen well enough to each other to fashion agreements.

Prior to the car crash, our family would gather for visits quarterly at mom and dad's home. In quiet moments when our parents were elsewhere, over drinks on the porch or on the beach on a warm afternoon, my siblings and I discussed our parents. This included general thoughts about their aging and what might lie ahead for them and us. We had naively assumed that our dad would be healthy and capable of independent living for a long time after the death of our mom, who was ill and whom we assumed would die first. We fell into the trap of dismissing the need to talk more about him . . . mostly because it was not easy to do so and we found his silence and wall of privacy off-putting. So we rationalized. Dad was an active, self-reliant, grounded man who lived in the same home for 20 years and still resided in the village of his birth. He was quite familiar with his environment. "Dad would be fine," we concluded, as we turned our attention to our mom.

Perhaps you too view your parents as healthy and capable of independent living. You think there's no need to talk today about a future when a parent's health declines, and he or she is less capable of that independence. Why rock the boat? Why initiate a conversation about the future when the family's having such a good time together? It might alter the mood completely, right? Our avoidance of Family Speak, even in the name of respecting a parent, inhibited our transitions with dad and each other. In the absence of such necessary preparatory conversations, we made decisions about dad's care only while he was in great physical pain, highly medicated, and unable to think clearly, let alone come up with a coherent and detailed plan for his own care.

Avoidance of Family Speak like ours is a common theme among those I counsel regarding their parents' changing situations. Many panic, fear becoming disrespectful if they are assertive, and delay an important discussion for another day. Below are three stories depicting very different Family Speak scenarios. Each one reminds us of the importance of talking sooner rather than later with a parent about his or her needs.

## Unfinished Business I

Dick and I chitchatted over pretzels and coffee while flying across the country. He was soon telling me about his dad, who was 82 and had recently fallen and broken his hip. His father was in a nursing home undergoing physical therapy but would be released soon. He was healthy enough to be independent, but he needed supervision. Dick's mom was gone and his sister's hands were full with her own family, which left Dick contemplating the possibility of bringing Dad into his home. The very thought of it made him nauseous!

Dick had always been afraid of his dad. When he was a boy, whatever he said was attacked as wrong or stupid, so eventually he didn't say much at all. It was easier that way. His dad criticized him for that, too, and there seemed to be no way for Dick to please him. This angered him, to the point that he distanced himself from his dad and in effect wrote him off. Since the death of Dick's mom, they had barely exchanged a word. How could his dad move in with him now? Dick was sure he would find fault with everything— from his choice of TV shows to his cooking and housekeeping style. Every time Dick considered talking to him, he saw himself as a little boy again, anxious to please, eager for his dad's respect.

During our conversation, and with a bit of prodding, Dick recognized that his dad might have changed over the years, especially in the last few months, after his fall. At the prospect of having to live in a nursing home, dad's need for control might have given way to a new sense of vulnerability. Perhaps it had not occurred to him that his son would one day have to care for him. Dick realized that, in reality, his dad no longer had the ability to hurt him. The son's sense of self-worth didn't need to be tied to his dad's lack of respect for him.

## Points to Ponder

Two issues stand out in this story. First, I often hear comments from mature adults—men and women alike—who fear talking with their parents in an authoritative manner. This is a testament to how powerful parents seem to their children, whether they know it or not. Kids grow up and find their own power base away from the family, but they rarely challenge their family system to claim their adult status with their parents. A wife will notice that her husband is different when they visit his family. He's not the in-charge guy she knows. A husband will be surprised when his wife caters to her mother and rarely makes decisions when she visits her mom's house. It's so unlike the confident woman he married.

You probably have your own version of the going-home story. Moms and dads are always the heads of the family. In order to honor their status, we, as adults, often tuck our own authority into a dark inner closet while visiting them. The more we've kept our wise adult selves out of potentially unsettling conversations with them, the harder any conversations on aging will be some day. Dick distanced himself, never risked standing up to his dad, and paid the price that unfinished business carries. It was with great trepidation that he initiated an adult conversation with his dad.

Second, I can't count the number of times clients approached their elderly parents with a long internalized desire for "respect" as they would like to receive it. Dick wants his dad to respect him, but what does that actually mean? Does he want dad to say "good boy" or "I'm proud of you"? It would be great if our parents could see our strengths and qualities as adults. But, as harsh as this may sound, many of them never will! When our personalities, lifestyles, and adult choices are similar to a parent's personality, lifestyle, and choices, it becomes easy to "see" and "be seen." Yet if we live life on different planets, so to speak, making choices far outside the comfort zone of a parent, asking for respect may be asking for the impossible. What we *can* ask for and hopefully receive is a willingness to let each other's distinctiveness contribute to productive Family Speak.

We have the ability to celebrate the "self" of all family members without necessarily appreciating their unique contributions to the world. For example, my family is happy that I'm happy and that I enjoy my career. None of them has been to counseling, and no one is interested in any of my clinical tales. They only want to know that all is well with me. Should I be offended? Early on in my career, I admit to having been hurt on occasion. Someone would ask a question about my therapy world and I would think briefly, "Oh, good, they're interested in how I work with people." When it became clear that I had misunderstood and the query was momentary, I came away sad. It didn't occur to me, until many years into my own adulthood, that my family respects me for various aspects of my unique self. As long as I don't need them to validate my personal gifts or honed skills, I can open my mind and heart to what they do see and cherish about me.

This type of situation may apply to some of you as well. It applies to Dick. From a child's place in his heart, he seems to want an affirmation that his dad may never be able to give. If Dick surrenders that desire, he might be better able to recognize and enjoy what his dad does cherish about him.

Dick's upcoming Family Speak with his dad at the rehab center may need to happen before either one of them can talk about other issues, including his dad's desires for health care as he weakens. They will have to talk sooner rather than later about those changing needs. This will be the starting place for them, as they learn more about each other—perhaps for the first time.

## Unfinished Business II

Dina's story has haunted me for year. She was emotionally and verbally abused by her father in her early adolescence, particularly after her mom died. In his eyes, she could do nothing right. His marriage to her mother included many nit-picking spats. She didn't do much right in her husband's eyes, either. Yet, when she died so young, he was devastated. He felt incapable of parenting their children without her. He worked hard, he drank hard, and he was tired at the end of the day. Dad often took his frustrations out on Dina, his oldest daughter. His unrelenting criticism left deep scars.

Dina's dad turned to his brother, who was several years his junior and not married, for companionship. They watched ballgames and drank beer together most weekends.

On at least one of these occasions, Dina was sexually abused by her uncle. She held her dad accountable for this outrageous experience. When confronted, her father downplayed his own rough, acerbic, and devaluing treatment of Dina and denied his brother's rape. The cognitive dissonance rattled her brain and kept her furious. "What should I do?" she often asked. Why wouldn't her dad believe her, even if he couldn't remember the incident? She left home bitter and confused.

After a painful life that included an inability to sustain a healthy marriage, after three tries over twenty years, she matured to the point where she was ready to seek professional help. In therapy, she wept uncontrollably week after week until she had emptied her soul of tears. As the tears receded, bitterness ebbed as well.

Dina's dad, by this time very ill and in a nursing home, had an epiphany of sorts. He missed his first-born and realized that he had alienated her with his sharp tongue. One day, he gathered up his courage and left her a phone message. Would she come and visit? Dina never answered his voicemail. For two years, she wouldn't consider seeing him. When her siblings nudged her to visit him, she refused. What was there to say? She could not have him indict her again.

Recently, Dina told me she was ready for the visit. "Why now?" I asked. "Well," she explained, "there are two reasons. First, dad calls every couple of weeks and leaves a tender message, and his words are really beginning to touch my heart. So maybe he won't be hurtful if I go to the nursing home. And second, I want a healthy relationship with a man. I think I need to see dad to put some closure on my past. I'm growing fonder of my new guy and don't want to mess up this relationship, too." It was critical to her to free herself from old, conflict-heavy baggage.

Dina's dad beamed when he saw her and burst into tears. He cried for several minutes before he could find his voice. He whispered "I love you" and "I've missed you." He told her that he was sorry for all the horrible things he'd said to her when she was young. Yes, he remembered those exchanges and yes, they were hurtful, and he wanted her to know that they had little to do with her. He was an unhappy man in an unhappy marriage. Dina was feisty; she looked like her mom; she was an easy target.

Once Dina's dad started talking, he continued for an hour. He had hurt Dina's mom in the same way. When her mom died in her early 40s of a rare form of breast cancer, he had forever lost the opportunity to tell his wife he was sorry. He drank away his sorrows.

Over the years, Dina's father had grown bitter toward Dina. He twisted the stories around in his mind, seeing himself as the injured party and maintained his victim stance. Dina should come to *him*, he thought. *She* abandoned him. *She* should apologize. More recently, though, lying in the nursing home, with many hours to think and no alcohol in his blood, he had time to reflect on his role in her life. He regretted having been so stubborn, not reaching out to her, not telling her how very sorry he was during the last 25 years. And now . . . here she was at his door. God had answered his prayers.

Dina's father never did acknowledge the rape. Maybe he really didn't know about it, maybe he was drunk at the time, and maybe he had truly forgotten their exchanges about it. Dina wasn't sure. She was, however, absolutely certain that her dad was sorry for his treatment of her as a teenager. He took her hands in his and told her through misty eyes that he didn't want to be separated from her ever again. "Please come back," he cried. As Dina shared her story, she too misted over. "He told me three times that he loved me," she said. It wasn't all that she wanted, but it was what her dad was able to give. Dina let it be enough.

After that first brave encounter, Dina visited her dad weekly until he died, only a few months later. She joined her siblings in planning the funeral and saying goodbye.

## Points to Ponder

The father's hunger for his daughter, whom he really loved despite his irresponsible way of showing it, and the illness that threatened his life compelled him to leave Dina messages regularly. Even if she never responded, he could be confident that she was hearing his messages. It was all he could do. Eventually, it worked.

Dina went to visit her dad when she was ready, when she had a clean heart, and only when she could listen to him with an open mind. She was blessed with a sincere apology, even though it did not address her inmost injury. So be it, she said to herself, because she returned regularly to be with her dad to the end. Two months cannot repair a lifetime wound, but it can allow forgiveness to free two hearts. Love came to life again before her dad's death.

If you struggle to connect with an estranged parent before he or she dies, allow the sacredness of life to permeate your protected heart and free you to find peace in the moment. You probably don't need your parent to make up for the past right now. It's over. Yet, you may need the time you spend with him or her to complete your grieving for the wounds you've carried for so long. Your parent may or may not reach out to you or apologize; he or she is a flawed human being on life's journey. You may bring grace just by showing up. Ultimately, if meeting with an alienated parent is on your path, you will know what to do at that moment. Take no expectations with you, only a peaceful heart. It will be enough.

## Next-Door Grandma

Neil and Cindy lived next door to his widowed mom for many years. Thanks to Neil's foresight, he and his parents had discussed potential living arrangements for the surviving parent after the other passed on. Because they could speak candidly with each other, Neil heard his parents' desires for autonomy despite any physical limitations that might arise. Cindy was brought in on the conversation, and together they figured out a way to ensure both safety and independence. All agreed to the purchase of adjacent properties when the time came.

After Neil's dad died, Neil and his mom researched properties and then agreed to the current arrangement. Because they could speak so freely with each other, whatever outcome emerged was going to be positive.

Neil's mother lived independently for about ten years, while Neil and Cindy kept an eye out for the unexpected. As aging gradually took its toll, they counted her pills, oversaw her bathing and laundry, brought her over to their home for several meals a week, and made sure her daily needs were met. Neil wouldn't have it any other way. Neither would Cindy. Their children also stopped in to visit grandma every day, shared their little stories, and loved her to pieces. All family members shared the duties, never felt put upon, and rarely tired of caring for her. Everyone grieved her death at 89 as a huge loss to them.

## Points to Ponder

I wish more families could brainstorm their way to creative options for themselves and their aging family members. In our mobile world, this is not always easy. Some of our elderly are rooted in a community in another state that they don't want to leave. Yet the care they need requires a local caregiver. Should they leave? Should they stay? The answers are unique to each family.

If aging can become a positive family experience for more of us, we will initiate conversations about future needs, long before parents and grandparents root themselves far from the rest of the family. Investing in property near family is only one option to consider. It worked for Neil and Cindy. Whatever the plan, the outcome could share these dimensions: Neil's mom never felt like a burden to anyone because she wasn't. She was loved deeply until the end, even when her needs escalated and her independence eroded. Neil and Cindy incurred some sacrifices to make his mom comfortable, but no sacrifice fell outside their comfort zone for her care.

Neil and Cindy are part of a new movement to bridge the gap in families generated by our mobile society. Younger seniors are talking with their older parents about living near each other, whether or not they enter a retirement community or reside next door. Through Family Speak they create their own family community to close the distance yet foster everyone's independence and well-being.

Since many of us cannot afford professional care for our parents, and our parents do not want to live with us, such community living is a respectful, fun, and loving option. Of course, it requires planning and that, in turn, requires talking to each other. . . .

Productive Family Speak unveils differences and expands choices. Can personality differences, personal inclinations, unique personal relationships, proximity, and specialized gifts call forth cooperation and compromise in your own family?

# 2

# So Many Choices
## *Honoring Differences and Expanding Options*

Family choices for care of aging members are growing. Many of us do not realize the range of options that have sprung up in the health care system. Often, we listen to a social worker's list of choices pre-disposed to assume the burden of responsibility. There was joy in my own family when we realized that dad had choices. Energized by options, we prepared to cooperate with each other for dad's long term needs.

On that January afternoon in 2005, mom had just received surprising news that she had stabilized after two years of debilitating chemo. Mom had told us she'd "do it," and so she did. "I won't die of cancer, Mare," she assured me once. "Just you wait and see."

Although an alert person, Mom never saw the vehicle speeding toward her and my father from the opposite direction. The crash flattened the passenger side of their car, and she was pronounced dead at the scene. Dad lay under the steering wheel for over a half hour while EMTs cut him out of the vehicle. He had broken legs and hips. He was medevaced to a hospital two hours from his nearest offspring in New Jersey.

During dad's month in intensive care, my siblings and I considered our choices for his treatment, including the facility where he would receive rehabilitative care. We asked for him to be transferred from New York to New Jersey, nearer to John, Jim, and Jeanne. Yet, the decision for placement was not in our hands. A bed had to open in a nursing home with suitable rehabilitation facilities near the city we'd designated. When the bed became available, the next part of dad's journey, and ours, began. We had no idea how long he would be in rehab. We did not know then whether he would ever walk again or be independent again. We weren't even sure he would live to decide. But we did know that we needed a contingency plan for the time when dad might be released from medical care to resume his life.

We had no plan in place. None of us had designed a home to house an invalid parent. We each had our personal disquieting assumptions about nursing homes and assisted living centers, and the implications of bringing a physically challenged parent into any of our living spaces. Then again, we knew so little about what real choices were out there. We based our thinking on early impressions of the rehab centers we explored prior to making our choice, anecdotes from movies, vivid stories we'd seen in investigative journalism reports, and hearsay from friends whose relatives had terrible tales to tell. One outraged family reported a parent's oozing bed sores caused by improper care; poorly trained staff had not bathed or dressed patients daily and left them alone for hours on end. As brothers and sisters, we gathered and began discussing options. Who could bring dad into their home?

Silence.

Our individual concerns about sharing our homes with dad mixed with fear: fear of losing the comfortable lives we had designed, fear of a spouse's reaction, and fear of our inability to have the compassion and patience needed for such care. Fear of other limitations too personal to disclose swirled inside us as well. And guilt, too, snuck in.

We were raised to honor our parents. Doesn't honoring a parent require sacrifice? Doesn't sacrifice require us to buck up and save dad from a system that might neglect him or even mistreat him? Doesn't sacrifice mean that we should ignore the costs to our own families—perhaps lost income, lost freedom, even strained marriages? What is the right choice? How do we maneuver the personal complexities attached to that simple question?

My family was ready to sacrifice as required, and we did. But we also needed to be practical about our choices and remain aware of the options. There is never one single way to care for those we love.

## Exploring Options for Your Family

Wading through so many unexpected emotions to make the best family choices for the elderly can be paralyzing for you and your family. You don't want to hurt your parents; you don't want to feel selfish; you and your family only wish to do the right thing, to the best of your abilities. Yet, exploring choices can often set off fires because all of us also have our own personal agendas. If your family hasn't developed productive Family Speak through the course of many years, making choices can stir up inner noise, misinterpretation, and unfair accusations. "Of course you'd want that option! It gets you off the hook for our parents' care!" Some people can end up feeling singled out, some can feel set up, and some can end up feeling trapped.

What to do?

In productive Family Speak, all choices are of equal value during the exploration phase. This phase is just that—

exploring and enumerating the choices available so that, when a decision is made later, it is made with the best and most complete information. The more potential options you can add to the list, the more readily you can eliminate the least favorable among them and focus on what works for the majority. What if one of the options does favor one sibling over another? What if someone thinks that his or her financial contribution should compensate for "being there." What if all the siblings, after consulting with physicians, support the need for antidepressant medication for a parent but the parent refuses to take any? What if all siblings but one support assisted living? In-home care still goes on the list, even if only one person supports the choice. Put all the questions on the list for discussion. There is no right or wrong at this point. Perhaps, through further Family Speak a creative option will emerge. This is the value of the exploration phase.

Talking together early on, preferably with your parents, is the key. Together, your family can develop a plan. Together, you can sift out the best options for your unique situation. This principle is critical to success, even if not everyone in the family chooses to participate in the discussions.

In our family, for example, the siblings spoke often and fully. Dad was consulted but only offered input on practical, in-the-moment decisions regarding doctor care. He did not help us on the long-term path.

Below are four stories of real women who have intervened in their parents' care. The choices they made differ, reflecting their unique circumstances. The way the conversations flow is based on their history, stemming from whether or not they were able to talk openly with each other.

## Long-Distance Daughter

Joan, a former client, lives in Ft. Lauderdale, Florida with her husband. Her mother, who suffered from Alzheimer's disease, lived in a nursing home in Boston, her hometown, near three of her children. Despite this physical distance, Joan, without her input, was named the primary caregiver and eventually executor of mom's estate.

Joan talked about her mom in loving ways. She visited her every three months, consulting with the doctors and spending time with the aides and nurses. When home, Joan phoned the nursing home weekly for updates and called her mom regularly. She made sure mom's hair was styled every Friday, that a manicurist was engaged occasionally, and that a physical therapist worked with her three times a week. Judging from this level of attentiveness and care, you would never know that longstanding discord had divided mother and daughter for decades. It was as though her mom's memory loss had wiped the slate clean.

The extended family, however, would never forget the deep-rooted friction between their mom and Joan that had ruined many a gathering. Their harsh and highly emotional fights were dreaded. Scars dug deep . . . until Joan's mom couldn't remember those times anymore.

In the last years, Joan found peace through her mom's childlike innocence and self-centered neediness. She experienced unexpected joy while tending to mom during those quarterly visits—a peace that was more tender and intimate than she had ever known with her.

Somehow, caring for her mom brought about a measure of healing for Joan. By the time her mother died, Joan had come to terms with her long-distance options and was confident that she had done her best given her circumstances.

After the unexpected death of their brother a year later, Joan and two of her sisters knew more healing was needed. They met for a long weekend to bury hatchets, seek and give forgiveness, and close the door on pain of the past. The third sister refused to attend the gathering. Perhaps it was for the best.

## Points to Ponder

Several issues are problematic in this family: a lack of productive Family Speak, the long-distance caregiving decision, and significant emotional discord. Inadvertently, Joan benefited from the choices made by others. Still this is a precarious position to be in. The land mines embedded in such an arrangement outweigh the potential benefits.

Joan and her siblings had not talked with their mom early on to discover her desires for care. It simply had never occurred to them to do so. When confronted with major responsibility, Joan's siblings passed the buck. They chose Joan, the eldest, as executor, to intervene on their behalf, even though she lived the farthest away and had been the innocent recipient of their mother's greatest rage. Joan reluctantly accepted the challenge. She was strong, she was capable, and she made it work. Perhaps Joan was weary of confronting her sisters; it's likely she gave up the fight.

Having placed herself as the go-to person, Joan set about finding the appropriate setting for her mom with little help from her siblings. They simply let her do whatever she thought best. Initially, the process worked well, for several reasons. First, consensus building was never necessary among the sisters. They deferred to Joan, even if they might periodically criticize her choices. Second, Joan's husband was supportive and respectfully deferred decision-making to her as well. Third, despite their difficult history, Joan had her mother's best interests at heart. Fourth, Joan was outspoken, clearheaded, and articulate. She became the stabilizing force. Doctors, nurses, attorneys, judges, and even her mom recognized Joan as the appropriate leader.

But despite numerous advantages, not all was well. One of Joan's sisters, who was mentally unstable, became bitter toward her and constantly tried to undermine her decisions. Often, when Joan left Boston, this sister raised complaints at the nursing home. She regularly questioned Joan's authority, and even took her to court, accusing her of stealing all of their mom's money. If Joan had moved to Boston, the intensity of that animosity might have increased, but, on the other hand, Joan could have exerted somewhat greater control.

To compensate for the intrusions of this sister, Joan developed a verbal relationship with the local judge, several attorneys, the nursing staff, and the administrative staff. Because there was no productive Family Speak during that time among the sisters, this discord and undermining of Joan's role continued until their mom's death. The courage that Joan displayed while her mother was alive was noteworthy. The meeting after their brother's death allowed the sisters to share their own stories with each other and break down their own misinterpretations and judgments. Forgiveness and love embraced them.

In my practice, I am disquieted by the amount of dissension I hear about in families struggling to choose a primary caregiver or decide who should have power of attorney for a parent. Most folks are better at telling others in the family what their role should be than fulfilling their own obligations: "If mom is moved near you, then you should visit her every day." "If you want dad to be near you, *you* should take over his bills, pills, and daily health needs." Sometimes, a family member buries her head in the sand and disclaims any responsibility: "You can count on me to share expenses, as needed, but I can't do anything to help. I've got a full plate. Besides, we all know that dad and I would fight every day over whatever decisions I make. No, thanks!"

If it is possible for families to talk frankly with each other about choosing power of attorney and selecting an executor early on (if a parent has not already named one), some of these disquieting conversations might be avoided. Family Speak might even be initiated by the parents who are writing their wills, living trusts, and health directives. Absent a parental lead, however, then a great question to ask is: "Mom and dad, who do you want to be executor to make major decisions for your care later on?" The more plans we, of either generation, can put in place ahead of time, the less jealousies, biases, and emotional battles dominate, distort, and detract from the tasks at hand.

## No Longer Waiting for Dad to Die

Paula, age 57, was a newly-divorced social worker living in Atlanta near her daughter's family when her mom died. Paula's only sister had died of cancer 15 years earlier. Dad was 88, residing in Virginia, and could not live alone. What should she do?

Paula chose to take a leave of absence to care for her dad in his large and comfortable home. Having grown up nearby,

Paula was familiar with the territory. Yet she and her dad were not prepared to live together. It would take the better part of the first year for them to get used to each other's ways. During that time, Paula went from being increasingly agitated around her dad to fearing she would wake to his death any day. One thing, though, made her fear bearable. It had an end in sight.

When a year came and went, Paula's dad had regressed to some extent, but he was still mobile. He wasn't ready to say goodbye. Suddenly, Paula felt trapped and angry. At times, she wanted to renege on her commitment. After all, she was young; could she continue to do what she was doing without going crazy? In a wise move, she decided to officially retire from her job, take a week's vacation, and regroup.

What happened next was extraordinary.

This younger daughter, who had never connected well with her dad, began to interact with him on an entirely different plane. Two divorces in life had taught her that she probably had "issues" with men. She began to deal with them.

The success in Paula's story is the fruit of her soul-searching style and thoughtful decision making. One day, she had an epiphany. She realized that she was not really living. Without having acknowledged it, she'd been waiting . . . waiting for her father to die.

This profound new awareness ushered in more meaningful conversations between them. Paula had tolerated her dad's annoying and intrusive idiosyncrasies, assuming he would not be with her long. Once awake to the possibility that they might be living with each other for several more years, Paula engaged him in a conversation about her different style and needs. Paula required more personal and physical space from dad. That was okay, her dad said. Paula needed vacations. That was okay, too, he said, but he wanted to live alone while she was away. That was not okay with Paula; he must be open to having a companion live with him during such times for safety.

Paula needed her dad to stop questioning her every move. That was hard for him to honor, but he tried. He needed Paula to tell him where she was going when she went out and when she'd be home. That would be fine, Paula said. He would appreciate Paula watching some TV with him at night; Paula agreed—sometimes. He asked Paula to trust him to take care of his personal needs unless he made a request of her. Paula grinned and agreed. She would not be joining him in the bathroom anytime soon.

These conversations occurred gradually over a three-month period and were quite tender. Paula's dad would never have initiated such talks. If Paula had not experienced her awakening, their relationship would have turned south a year earlier. She steered away from a dead end and into success.

Paula and her dad are approaching the end of their second year of sharing a home. Paula has made his space more homelike for herself. She's redecorated the upstairs, bought a new TV, and taken over the kitchen. She's found a part-time job, she volunteers at a stable, and she works out at a health club. Paula continues to develop healthy boundaries.

Paula's dad will never see her the way she wants to be seen—as a sharp, savvy businesswoman, as an independent, resourceful homeowner, and an excellent mother and grandmother—but he does love her, tells her so now, and thanks her often for being with him . . . words she's never heard before. If he steps over the line at times, it's usually because he's trying to make her a replacement for her mom (have cocktails with him at 5, watch his TV shows, know just by intuition what foods he *doesn't* like). Paula nips many of those requests in the bud.

This has been an important growing time for Paula. She doesn't regret it. Fear of confronting yet another death in her world is always in the back of her mind. Still, she is not the same person who moved in with her dad two years ago. She will handle what she needs to handle. As she might say, all is well.

## Points to Ponder

It's not uncommon for family members to "wait for" their parent to die. Perhaps this seems a shocking idea. Yet the caregiving experience is complex and exhausting for caregivers. They are honorable people and have volunteered to help out, but they too have lives, lives that all too frequently are dramatically disrupted during the caregiving time. They expect this temporary new arrangement to be just that—temporary.

Paula did not expect to be blessed by her dad's extended life. The gifts came as a huge surprise. The opportunity to live with her father in the midst of her maturity and his neediness benefited them both. They endured their version of a face-off during the first year, and both emerged changed for the better. As her dad adapted to her ways and began to appreciate her special womanly presence, Paula found a voice with dad, a voice I am confident will extend to other men should she choose to seek future intimate relationships.

You may be intrigued by what occurred in this family. Perhaps you, too, will go beyond whatever fixed relationship you've established with a parent and, at a deep level, find that certain something that he or she wants to share with you. In the beginning, it can be awkward, frustrating, and anxiety-producing. After a while, though, you, too, will likely make peace with the way your parent is and will continue to be. You'll enjoy their attempts to love you—not necessarily as you had expected to be loved, but in their own fashion. From so many who have crossed my path, I hear that the fruits of trying are sweet.

## Keeping a Spouse at Home—"I Can't Do That to My Husband"

Sandy lived about 150 miles from her folks. She anguished over her parents' situation. Her mom, Nancy (a friend of mine), was healthy, in her late 60s, but her dad, Bob, in his mid-70s, had Parkinson's disease. Bob begged Nancy to keep him in their home. Married for 45 years, Nancy loved her husband dearly, and honoring his request seemed to her the only option. They lived in the family home for three years as he rapidly deteriorated, requiring a great deal of care. Money grew tight, Nancy's health suffered, and her ability to invest energy as the primary caregiver waned.

Sandy helped as much as she could, calling her folks daily and visiting them every month, but care of her own little ones limited her travel. To top things off, she was now pregnant with her third child. So by necessity, Nancy carried the burden. Friends urged her to consider a nursing facility for her husband. "No. He doesn't want that. I can't do that to my husband," she had said often. Yet, during the periods when Bob had been rushed to the emergency room and had to stay in a hospital for a few weeks, Nancy smiled more, had more energy, and was visibly less anxious.

The family anguished over what appeared to them to be Nancy's loving but unwise decision and the effect it was having on her health. Sandy and her siblings would describe the merits of nursing home living as a means of giving their dad the kind of care that could sustain his dignity and give mom a reprieve, but Nancy could not hear it and tried other solutions. She hired caregivers to come in several days a week to help bathe and dress Bob, she welcomed friends who offered to sit with him while she shopped or went to church, and she enjoyed timely breaks through the kindness of other family members. Even with this extra level of help in home health care, however, she wore out.

When Bob died, the family felt enormous sadness at the loss of a special man, but their sadness was fused with relief. Nancy, however, did not feel relief. After he was gone, she was emotionally exhausted and cried through many lonely nights. Despite her children's constant efforts to fill her time with activities with their families, feelings of loss dominated her for almost two years. Eventually, however, Nancy regained her health and reconnected with friends and activities in the community.

Was keeping her husband at home the right thing to do? Her children weren't at all convinced. For Nancy, however, it definitely was the right choice. She could not have done otherwise.

### Points to Ponder

Nancy made her choices from two significant planes. First, her husband begged her to keep him in their home despite the progression of his disease. Second, their savings were not sufficient to keep him in an expensive facility for several years. We cannot argue with the second of these realities. The first is questionable. As soon as Nancy's health became compromised by their caregiving choices, she would have benefited from reconsidering the promise she made her husband. She might have promised to visit him every day, if he chose a professional care facility. She might have told him that the seriousness of his needs and the weariness of her body were inhibiting the quality of their lives. She might have considered taking a part-time job to help defray the costs of the extra care. More generally, she might have helped her husband see that professional care was not a death sentence.

Such exploratory talks never happened. Understandably, Bob, facing a debilitating disease, was frightened for his future and depended on his wife's support in all ways each day. Early long-term care facilities had a bad reputation; in his mind, nursing homes connoted loneliness, isolation, poor care, and death before death. Though Bob was not good at articulating his emotions, Nancy could read fear in his blue eyes whenever she broached the subject. She could not dishonor her husband and go against his wishes. Time would probably be short. She would stay the course, no matter what others said.

It's likely that, if she had to face the same sets of choices today, Nancy would have approached the situation differently. Long-term care facilities are gradually becoming more affordable—the $60,000 annual fee for luxury living is not the only choice — and families with modest means are now able to explore a wider range of options. Conditions will continue to change to accommodate the growing needs of our aging society.

Even though her choice was not one that others might have made, Nancy didn't have her head in the sand. She knew the situation, she talked with others, and she listened well. She was informed and did what seemed best for her at the time. If Nancy erred, it was in minimizing the effects of long-term, in-house care on herself as a caregiver. She may have thought that with resolve and great love, she had the ability to withstand upcoming challenges. Yet how could she prepare adequately for her reactions to a loved one's physical failings? How could any caregiver prepare for the emotional toll a family member's inability to verbalize, hold a fork, bathe, walk, or do more than gaze through eyes reflecting fear and sadness would have on them . . . day after long, painful, and exhausting day?

In Nancy's case and others like it, we have to honor the choices of those who are determining the care. We can suggest that the road will not be easy, that other options may be better for all concerned, but if the Nancys of the world cannot open their minds to loving a different way, then we have no choice but to prepare ourselves to become caregivers of the caregivers when their needs emerge . . . as they will.

## The Freedom to Change Your Mind

Some adult children don't believe they have any choice when caring for their aging or ill parents. They absorb enormous consequences without seeking options—and usually without family conversations. Others attempt to make healthy decisions for the greater good but ultimately succumb to pressure anyway. When you realize how much the world has changed in just a few decades, you start to see how options that used to seem unpalatable have become attractive. This will give you a better way to deal with guilt if, as sometimes happen, you are not able to honor a promise never to use a nursing home.

Mary was married with five young children, a full-time homemaker, while her husband traveled four days a week for his job. When her 70-year-old parents became incapacitated due to her dad's ill health, her mom's broken hip, and poor eyesight for both, she knew that they could no longer live alone in their New York apartment, fifty miles from Mary's New Jersey home. So she helped them sell their belongings and moved them to a nursing home in her hometown. She agonized over the decision not to force her children to share bedrooms to make room for grandma and grandpa. Although she visited them several times a week, her father looked at her with the most pained expressions on his face. He simply could not believe that his only daughter would do such a thing to him. Her choice felt like a knife to his heart. He never said a word to her. But then, as is so often the case, he didn't have to.

He died within a year. Guilt exploded in Mary's heart and shaped her next decision. She brought her mother home. Her mother was still mending her broken hip; she was also half blind, incapable of bathing herself, incontinent, and needy in numerous other ways. For the next 18 months, and with the assistance of home health care, Mary tended to her as best she could, but her best was not enough. Her marriage suffered, her kids began to act out, and her own health became compromised. Anxiety and exhaustion dominated her life. She shared her feelings with her husband and some friends, but nonetheless she trudged on, faithful to her mother until the end. She had been a good and loving daughter, but her choice almost did her in.

## Points to Ponder

Mary was not able to stand firm on her choice for her mom and dad. Given the responsibilities she already shouldered at home, the nursing home had been an excellent decision. But when her dad died, Mary caved in. Guilt decided the outcome of this story, the effect of a long-standing family power play. Mary's mom had often given her grandchildren clothing and gifts, she'd lent the family money when finances were tight, and she would take the older children on fun trips in the summer. When Mary thanked her for the help, her mom would say "Just take care of us when we're old." These words became a ball and chain for Mary any time housing discussions emerged. Her mom's unspoken message was clear: "Bring us into your home. Don't pawn us off on some nursing home. That's not taking care of us." This older couple was so convinced their daughter would care for them the way they wished to be taken care of that they were shocked when it didn't work out this way. Mary felt as if she had no choice; they were expecting the impossible.

Mary might have benefited from talking with professionals or friends who experienced similar binds. In her day (this was before 1990), she would have had to work much harder at building these conversations. Today, however, Mary could enjoy conversations with many on the same journey, and find significant support for holding her ground. She could meet others facing the same guilt-inducing choice. They could have helped her validate her limitations and stand her ground. The Internet, replete with blogs, chat rooms, and websites on aging would have been a tremendous resource for her. She could even lovingly offer a "second-best" choice, one that might eventually become acceptable even to her parents.

Mary would not be a lonely pioneer today, and she would have more attractive choices. Many people today are talking about the future with their still active yet aging parents, nursing homes are less foreboding, and TV ads invite us to plan for tomorrow today. Elderly facilities are less likely to be seen as places where someone goes to die, and they exude more of a home atmosphere. The décor and staff are welcoming: fresh flowers abound, cozy dining rooms invite conversations, special weekly activities provide fun distractions, and companions share the aging journey.

In hindsight, we can discern many options in the above stories. In each story, the family members made the best choices they could, given their circumstances. But they may not be the best or right choices for you. To expand your options today, you need to talk sooner rather than later, while appreciating the complexities involved in your reversing roles. Through the process, you will come to greater knowledge of your abilities and limitations as a caregiver; you only need to be at peace with them.

The value of candid conversations on these sensitive topics is never to be underestimated. What happens when you and your own family are not on the same page when you start talking?

# 3

# Candid Conversations

## *Trusting Each Other with the Truth— Even When It Hurts*

Theresa, age 72, was relegated to a wheelchair two years ago. She's survived well on her own in her handicap-accessible home. Still, she would agree that her peace of mind comes from knowing that her very helpful kids live nearby and keep close watch over her. Her son, Mike, in particular has showered her with attention and love. He's single and until recently has had extra time. A week ago, however, he was asked by his employer, a nationwide retail company, to transfer over 1000 miles away to open a new store. If he refuses, he'll lose his job. His company knows his situation, yet he is the only single manager they could entrust with this new endeavor. How does he tell his mom? How does he tell his sister? He dreads telling each of them. Mike scheduled a consult with me prior to telling his family the unwelcome news. Through a most candid conversation with his sister that occurred later that week, and some negotiating with his employer for monthly weekend visits home, Mike forged a plan that satisfied everyone.

Candid conversations can occur in every home, amongst every age group. You have probably struggled through your share of them, either initiating them or being asked to participate in them. They are the vehicle for discussing private and personal needs, for raising hurts and old wounds, for making changes in a family's way of relating to each other, and for clearing the air. Sometimes, we need to speak the truth, even if the other person doesn't want to hear our thoughts. Sometimes, in turn, we are the ones who need to hear the truth, even if it hurts.

Candid conversations with our parents about their care, living arrangements, or end-of-life decisions are made more difficult by taboos unique to each family. These talks call many of us outside our comfort zones. The topics that are traumatic and disquieting for my family may not be the ones that upset yours, but we all know, even without being told, what hot buttons control our own loved ones. And we know intuitively when we are pushing them. The emotional stakes are high.

My siblings and I attempted many frank conversations with our own parents over the years. Mom would always appreciate our candor regarding her situation, even when she felt offended. She was a good communicator, though, and touchy situations were usually resolved. Mom was protective of dad, however, insisting that she should be the go-between and prepare him for our needs or requests. Far too often, she would also be the one to report dad's responses. Sometimes, she would use the opportunity to cajole. Usually, it worked. But not regarding dad's boat . . .

Even after my father's recovery from rectal cancer at age 75, his faculties and adeptness at many activities, including captaining his 22-foot cabin cruiser, noticeably diminished. We saw it, and my brothers even compensated for it, but dad remained the captain. He would not let anyone relieve him at the helm. For four years, the family, especially mom, lived with serious concern whenever dad took the boat out alone.

When we shared our concerns with mom, she asked us not to mention them to dad. She'd talk with him, she told us. Another year passed. Perhaps she never did speak with him, or her words fell on deaf ears.

During the July 4th festivities one year, when dad wanted to take the boat out on the bay to view the fireworks, several of us refused to go, fearing his poor judgment and slow reaction time on the water. We also opted out of other summer rituals such as excursions across Long Island Sound. Still, Dad would still not surrender his captain's hat. On another occasion, while fishing with dad, my brother, Jim, quietly said, "Dad, you've had a great run with this boat. It's been the family treasure for 20 years. I know you don't like to hear this, but you are slowing down a little. Might you consider selling the boat soon or letting one of us take the helm?" He looked at Jim and said, "I'll know when it's time for me to hang up my hat. Until then, please be helpful or stay off the boat." He accepted no help because he could not acknowledge his limitations.

Other Family Speak conversations were attempted but failed. Eventually, at age 80, dad hung up his captain's hat and sold the boat. He said that he was tired and that mom needed more of his caregiving time. We let his pride carry the day. At least he was off the water.

Selling the boat ushered in old age for dad. Until then, he had held onto a sense of control and personal meaning. Protective to the end, mom begged us not to make a big deal of the sale. After years of many precious memories with the boat, though, I couldn't let it go. I wrote dad a poem for his birthday, had it framed, and called it "Ode to the Captain." He hung the poem in the foyer, an action that revealed his appreciation.

When dad recovered from his cancer, mom and he initiated candid conversations about their end-of-life desires. Apparently, the limitations brought on by aging and surrendering the boat were taboo topics, but wills, living trusts, and medical/health directives were not.

First, they discussed their wills and came to agreement on which of their children would take on greater or lesser responsibility in different areas. Second, they took their documents to an attorney for exactness, legalese, and official format. Third, they visited each of us that year and in person described to us what they wanted. Fourth, they secured a cemetery plot for the two of them that was attached to the one where dad's parents were interred.

These four little activities made an enormous difference for us. Mom and dad did not need our help with the pragmatic decisions for burial, will execution, and division of basic assets. We learned about their assets and what would be our share. My brother Jim, our official executor, and my brother John, his unofficial assistant, who shared power of attorney status with him, had signed the legal papers and were as prepared as anyone could be for the dreaded day. Both brothers were qualified to honor our interests. We trusted them.

A few years later, we engaged in two additional candid conversations with our dad. The first regarded mom's care during her second bout of cancer. We wanted mom's care to be a team effort. But he didn't want a team. He was the sole decision maker. He would gladly pass on whatever information we requested, but we would have no say on choices nor direct access to the doctors. I decided to nudge dad a bit while visiting. On a drive with him to the store one day I broached the team concept. I was told to mind my own business. He'd ask for help with mom if he ever needed it.

How dare I think that he was not capable of doing his job! Through my own filter, I felt criticized and heard the door slam shut. I never knocked on that door again.

After dad died, I realized two important aspects of the situation that fed dad's reaction. First, he had been preparing to become mom's caregiver for several years. He was ready for the job. Second, dad felt devalued when I suggested he might want the family's help. He needed us to value his abilities as a caregiver. My suggestion accomplished the opposite. There were no further talks on mom's care. Truth be told, one of dad's greatest life accomplishments centered around his gentle caring for mom during those four years. I had inadvertently missed an opportunity to acknowledge him.

The second candid conversation occurred shortly after mom's death while dad was in intensive care. He was adamant that we would not have a funeral for mom until he could attend. We knew that dad would be confined to bed for weeks, at the very least. "Dad," my brother Bill ultimately said to him, "you will need surgery this week and may be laid up for a long time. Please allow us to have a funeral. We really need to complete this ritual for the family." Dad looked so very sad. Then, caught in a real bind, he bent to logic. "Okay, but I don't want you to bury mom until I can be there."

Done.

We agreed readily to that request, knowing that mom's ashes could remain at the funeral home as long as necessary.

Dad was a hard man to engage in a deeper level of dialogue, but we kept trying. It's the trying that is important. Sometimes, receivers like our dad need to "cook" with the ideas for a while, and a second or third go-around may bear more fruit. After awhile, we had successful conversations with dad. When his own illnesses made professional care necessary, we had more say in the decisions. Perhaps we had paved the way; perhaps he softened. We'll never know.

You may share similar concerns when talking candidly with your parents: Do you initiate a conversation about growing older with them when you observe a need, or do you wait for them to bring up the subject? Do you comment when they are well or hold off until illness compromises the conversation?

Below are four examples of candid conversations. Perhaps one of them is similar to those that occur in your own family.

### Opening the Door—The First Conversation

Ed is a friend with whom I shared my early thoughts for this book. He had the following discussion with his parents on his next visit home.

*Ed*: Mom and Dad, could we talk about some important stuff?

*Mom*: Sure, son. Is anything wrong?

*Ed*: No, nothing's wrong with me. It's you I worry about. I'm becoming more concerned about you both, now that you're getting older. Please hear me out, and then think about what Sis and I need to do when you can no longer live on your own. I've been reading a lot lately about living wills and trusts, about health directives, and I've been pondering how I could help you, if either of you were to get sick. You guys live on 40 acres, all by yourselves, and you're 85 years old. I want you to be realistic . . .

*Dad*: We're doing just fine, son. You know we made out our wills years ago. You and your sister are listed as the beneficiaries on all our savings. We're both healthy . . .

*Ed*: No, you're not, Dad. You recently had your third skin cancer removed and you're more forgetful. Both of those things frighten me. Mom is always going to the doctor, and she's on lots of meds. Her legs aren't strong anymore, and I noticed, even today, that she has a hard time walking. Even you move a lot slower than you used to, Dad; I see it every time I visit. You won't come to Virginia anymore, and rarely take the hour's drive to Sis's house. These things are serious.

*Mom*: What should we do, other than what we're already doing?

*Ed*: I need to tell you this next part, and it's hard. I don't want to hurt you. But you know me. I don't handle sickness well. I wouldn't manage your physical care needs with ease. My bedside manner would deteriorate. Don't shake your head, Mom. It's true. Leaving my home would also be a challenge for me. I haven't retired yet. I have commitments. Still, my home stuff isn't as important as the fact that I am not a caregiver. It won't happen. Sis has four kids and a husband. Is she going to come here? Are you going to go live with her, both of you, or one of you? Have you talked with each other about these possibilities, let alone talked with Sis?

*Mom*: No, we thought that since you're nearing retirement and, until recently, single, that you'd come here to be with us. We want you to have this place after we're gone anyway.

*Ed*: I'd be more unkind than helpful. It's not that I don't love you. I just don't have the stamina for dealing with the medical stuff, the intimate care, and all those kinds of things. I could cook and clean and mow the lawn . . . but I couldn't give you the kind of personal care you may need in the future, the care you may both need at the same time.

**Dad**: So, what would make you feel better?

**Ed**: Well, several things. First of all, just think about all this. I know it's hard to swallow, but please consider this the beginning of a conversation, not the end of one. Secondly, could you write down your desires for extended health care, if you become unconscious and are not expected to live? Could you share with Sis and me what you'd like for your funerals? Do you want to be buried or cremated? If you want to be buried, where might that be? I realized recently that I don't know the answers to these questions. We've never talked about this personal stuff at all. Third, divide your assets. You have many treasures here. Write down what you want Sis to get and what you want me to get. It will make it so much easier for us later on.

**Mom**: Well, I want Sis to get all my jewelry.

**Ed**: Of course you do. Write it down.

**Mom**: What do you want?

**Ed**: I want what you want me to have . . . that's all! Except the Hummels, and that special picture you painted many years ago. If you don't put my name on it, then later on it could go . . . anywhere. I'd hate that.

**Dad**: We could do some of this, Ed. But since we're talking this way, I have to say something. Now that you're married again, I'm concerned about what happens with the monies we've saved. Now, I like your wife a lot . . . but . . . one of the reasons I haven't put anything on paper is that I don't want her family to get our assets.

**Ed**: Dad, that won't happen. We signed a prenuptial agreement months before the wedding. You know that. It protects you. And she wants to protect her own assets for her children, too. You have nothing to worry about on that end.

*Mom*: Okay, that answers that question. But we have so much stuff, I don't know who should get what.

*Ed*: That's the reason to start talking. Ask me if I want something; ask Sis. Start your lists . . . and then when the time comes, we'll all be on the same page. Who do you want to be executor of your estate?

*Dad*: Well, we can't ask you because you live out of state.

*Ed*: That's not true, Dad. There might be papers to sign, but you can have whomever you want become the executor. You have to make that decision, though. It's very important. Talk with your attorney. If you don't want to ask Sis or me to do it, ask him to do it for you. You have choices here. Make some and put them in writing. That's the important part . . . put them in writing!

*Mom*: This is overwhelming, Ed. And I hadn't thought at all about not being able to live here on this property. We love it so.

*Dad*: Those senior care places—they won't be right for us.

*Ed*: Maybe they're *not* right for you. Maybe you can use some of your assets to hire someone to live in with you to care for you. Medicare would send visiting nurses out periodically depending on your needs. You have options.

*Mom and dad in unison*: No live-ins!

*Ed*: Maybe not . . . but maybe it's a better choice than some of the others.

*Dad*: We've saved our money for a long time for you and Sis. We won't spend it on a live-in.

*Son*: Dad, we don't need your money—neither of us do. Spend your money to live well and live longer. That would please us the most.

## Points to Ponder

This discussion continued for the better part of an hour and resumed later in the day over cocktails before dinner. It was a most intimate time for this family, the kind of Family Speak they rarely shared. Ed's parents didn't address all of the son's points in the dialogue, but they addressed enough of them to consider the conversation worthwhile. Ed set a clear, yet disquieting, boundary for his parents. He was honest, and his love for them guided his words. It bore fruit. Since Ed addressed his parents so forthrightly about their potential needs and his own limitations, the level of discussion among them has deepened. His mom told Ed that they are sorting through their treasures and putting their wishes on paper.

The written word is very powerful. It's also clear and definitive. Many families break apart over what "mom wanted me to have" or what "you know dad said would be mine." This becomes tug-of-war material after the fact. Parents do their children a favor by writing down their wishes—in detail.

When I hear of conversations like the one above, I'm reminded that parents are only human, and perhaps haven't a clue about how to plan for their future or talk with their kids about their treasures. Getting started is the challenge. Ed was lucky—his parents opened up remarkably well. If you are met with resistance, do try again in the near future. You will have invited family to consider the questions you raise and the limitations you bring as a potential caregiver. They will ponder your words carefully, even if it takes them a long time to respond to you.

Perhaps the conversation will go the other way— your parents may wish you to know *their* desires and their concerns. They may have requests that you find hard to swallow. If you allow the conversation to start, though, you too might benefit from pondering their thoughts without becoming unduly reactive. The earlier Family Speak begins, the longer families have to discern their choices.

Candid conversations mean just that—being frank but respectful and letting truth reign.

### "I've Never Stood Up to Mom Before."

This was a conversation between a friend of mine and a trusted friend of hers.

*Pat*: How's your mom?

*Carol*: Don't ask! I'm so frustrated with her this week. You know her health is failing and at 90, she still forgets that she's limited. On Monday, Mom announced that she's going to Texas for a month . . . for the birthday party of an old friend. The doctors don't think it's a wise choice, and neither do I. Mom's frequent falls are a problem; travel isn't a good idea. When I told Mom that I couldn't break from work to take her, she declared that she would go alone.

*Pat*: Please tell me you won't let her do it!

*Carol*: No, I wont. Yet, it's challenging for me to say "no" to her. At 60, I still feel like a guilty little girl when I do.

*Pat*: Could she find a traveling companion?

*Carol*: We've been arguing over that one all week. She's adamant about not wanting a caregiver to go with her. Her plan is a pipe dream, but when I told her so, she overrode me and phoned in her RSVP.

*Pat*: I'm concerned for you now, Carol. I know your mom's stubborn. I'm afraid that you'll give in and let her run right over you. I'm saying this as your friend. My words may be hard to hear, but I think you need to toughen up. Didn't she travel with her neighbor before? Perhaps the neighbor could be a pinch hitter for you this time.

*Carol*: I don't know! Mom is so determined to do her own thing. Did I tell you she even plans my evenings? After sitting all day, she's ready for an outing when I get home from work. When I tell her I'm tired, her lips curl out and I feel guilty. What if she dies right after I say 'no' to her? Then, I would die of sheer guilt.

*Pat*: I'm sorry. You don't want to rock the boat, do you?

*Carol* (crying): It's hard to think of losing her. With David gone for ten years now, and without children, I can feel hamstrung when mom and I disagree.

*Pat*: But you do a lot for your mom. She's blessed to have you.

*Carol*: Sure, I do, mostly because I can't say "no."

*Pat*: Not so! Remember the trip you and I took last year? Even though your mom resisted, we left her in the care of a friend at home. And that worked out all right, don't you think?

*Carol*: I do take a stand sometimes, don't I?

*Pat*: The way I see it, your mom seems to accept your needs when you are firm.

*Carol*: I suppose so. Only this time, she's intent on attending this party.

*Pat*: Why don't you think about this differently? Perhaps the problem here is not mom's stubbornness, but the way you react to her. She's only doing what's worked well for her over the years. Sometimes she pouts and you cave! Isn't that a poor substitute for respect?

*Carol*: You're right. Thanks for the nudge. Mom has a friend who's retired, and she's has offered to help. I'll give her a call.

## Points to Ponder

Sometimes it's awkward to stand up to our parents. If, for example, you work outside the home, you might interact with folks all day long in a competent, mature, decision-making mode and then forget how to do so with mom and dad.

With Carol, and perhaps some of you, three issues dominate. The first is inescapable. Carol's mom is her last surviving family member. Letting go is painful. Deciding not to rock the boat for any reason may seem like a logical and loving option. Clearly, though, such a choice puts the caregiver in a terrible bind. Exhaustion soon sets in. If a person caters to another person's needs while ignoring her own, she will wear out. Self-care is the foundation of being really helpful to others. It requires people to set boundaries that make sense in order to be present for the long haul.

The second issue may be that of an unhealthy lifelong response to conflicting desires in families: defer to others or deal with the guilt of saying no. It's an adaptive trait learned in childhood. Perhaps Carol never felt free to be herself and stand her ground. For whatever her reasons, she did take self-care steps, but she attached guilt to these choices over the years. It is sad to make healthy choices for oneself and not be able to claim the rewards for them. Fortunately for Carol, the situation is forcing her to free herself . . . in her case, to be free from this self-prescribed prison when she talks with her mom about their differing wishes. Unless she frees herself, guilt will destroy her long before death claims her mom's body.

The third issue emerges from the conversation between Pat and Carol. They are friends, and Pat feels empowered to speak candidly with her friend. Carol listens well and receives the nudges her friend offers. Sometimes, such comments from friends sound harsh and unloving. Carol could have dismissed her friend as someone who "just didn't understand" the situation. But Pat *did* understand the problem and felt compelled to steer her friend toward an appropriate course. What would you do if a friend of yours seemed stuck, but perhaps didn't want your unsolicited advice?

## Asking for Details: "Mom, What Do You Want to Wear in the Coffin?"

Father Joe, a friend of mine, visited his mom in the hospital every three weeks. It was the best he could do under the circumstances. He was the lone priest in a parish some three hundred miles from his mom's home. On one particular visit, Fr. Joe had talked with his mother's doctor and learned that she didn't have much time left. He took a deep breath, looked up to the heavens uttering a quick prayer, and opened her door. Hiding behind his famous smile, Fr. Joe went to his mom's side, held her hand, and began:

*Fr. Joe*: You look a little tired today, Mom.

*Mom*: You're so subtle, son. I know you talked with the doctor a little while ago. I am weary—and ready to go.

*Fr. Joe*: Yes, I talked with the doctor. I know this part of life will end soon. I love you, Mom. I will miss you so very much.

*Mom*: I know, Son. I'm okay, though. I'm not even afraid, you know? I thought I would be, but I'm not. I'm ready for whatever is ahead.

*Fr. Joe*: God is ahead, Mom. I don't know what that will be like, but I'm sure it will be wonderful. Mom, I know we've talked about what you'd like for your funeral, but is there anything else you want from me that you haven't told me? Like, a silly question, maybe, but I'm a guy so I wouldn't know these things. What do you want to wear in the coffin?

*Mom*: Hmmm . . . I have two dresses, the lavender one I wore when we went to Israel, remember?

*Fr. Joe*: I certainly do.

*Mom*: And the green one that everyone says makes my eyes look bright.

*Fr. Joe*: Which one do you want?

*Mom*: You pick. I don't even care if you put one on me at the viewing and the other one when they want to bury me. . . . Whatever you want.

*Fr. Joe*: Okay, I'll think about it. Know that I love you, mom. I'll see you tomorrow.

The next day, Fr. Joe again visited his mom before returning to his parish. He spent the better part of their time together reminiscing about sweet memories and praying with her. She told him how much she loved him and was proud of him. She hoped he'd stay in contact with his brothers. He promised he would. As Fr. Joe prepared to leave, his mom spoke up.

*Mom*: So, what did you decide?

*Fr. Joe*: About the dress? I picked the lavender one because it has sweet memories of our special trip attached to it.

*Mom*: Good choice! I love you. You've been a good son. Pray for me every day.

*Fr. Joe*: How could I not? I'll remember you in that lavender dress, and it will always bring a smile to my face.

This meeting was anything but light for Fr. Joe. He had buried his dad a few years back, his sister died shortly thereafter from a house fire, and more recently his only other sibling had succumbed to a heart attack. He was not ready to bury his mom, too. Saying goodbye was a painful conversation, lavender dress and all. His mom, protecting him to the end from his deeper emotions, set the tone. She didn't know that when he got back to his car, he put his head on the steering wheel and wept like a baby. "It's not fair, God. It's just not fair. You've asked so much of me these last five years. I can't take any more right now."

Fr. Joe didn't know that when he left, his mom asked a caregiver to put her prayer book and her rosary beads in her hands. She could not read anymore; her eyes could not focus for very long. She could not move her fingers; they were stiff and frozen. But she could hold her holy items and pray quietly. "Be with my boy in all things, God," she prayed. "He'll have a tough time when I'm not here. Bless his work and bring him good friends. Thank you for the life you've given me, for the family you've given me, for the husband you hold in your arms—and who waits even now for me. I am not afraid. I am ready to enter into your arms when you want me. Amen."

## Points to Ponder

So far in this section on candid conversations with our aging parents, the exchanges have ranged from an early dialogue revealing inevitable changes, to middle stage assertions against an aging mother's demands, to a son's compelling goodbye to his mom. Each stage exposes different, often difficult aspects of our truth, forcing us to face head-on those parts of us we've buried. Ed found a firmness and candor with his stubborn parents that was not his normal style. Carol pushed through guilt, found her voice, and faced the consequences a longstanding lack of assertiveness had imposed on her relationship with her mom. Fr. Joe released his emotional floodgates in the privacy of his car, mixed as his grief was with a heavy fear of becoming the last man standing in his family.

In the last exchange retold below, the truth remained unuttered in a father's throat just days before his death.

## When the Door Slams Shut: "I Won't Talk. Don't Ask Me."

Denise is a small business owner whose shop I frequent. She related the following conversation to me.

*Denise*: Dad, can we please talk about what you want when the end comes?

*Dad*: I really don't want to.

*Denise*: Dad, this is not easy; I need your help. What do you want for your funeral? I don't know where to start.

*Dad*: (Tears and more tears.)

*Denise*: Dad, I don't want to make you cry—I just don't know what to do or what you want.

*Dad*: I can't. I can't talk about it. Do whatever you want.

### Points to Ponder

Some of us are never able to put our feelings and needs into words. If we have spent a lifetime not doing so, they will clog in our throats at the end. This dad had *never* talked with his daughter about his joys or fears in life. They had developed a rather superficial relationship, based on activities and events. When dad's final days approached, Denise hoped against hope that her dad would be able to let her in. Her frustration and sadness are evident when that didn't happen.

Denise told me that her father was Jewish, and therefore cremation was not an option. Beyond that, she didn't have a clue about what to do. We discussed contacting a Rabbi to let him walk her through the proper rituals. She did this and all went well, although she would have preferred to have her dad help her out with his desires.

Denise's dad did try to talk heart-to-heart with her. His tears were evidence of strong emotion. Yet after a life of self-protection, he couldn't let himself talk through the tears. Ultimately, all Denise could do was back off and honor her dad, whichever way the path unfolded.

Her dad's girlfriend offered Denise the following explanation after his death: "Your dad told me that he felt enormous fear surge through him when you mentioned death. He faced his disease and made peace with how it had robbed him of his golden years. It was God he feared. He couldn't find words for that." If Denise's father wouldn't talk about his fear, then peace would elude him and fear would choke him . . . as, in fact, it did.

The ability to enter into candid conversations is a prerequisite to maneuvering together through the maze of professional care, if or when a family member's limitations require extraordinary help. Have you thought about the ways your own family could manage a time when a loved one might need this higher level of attention?

# 4

## Experiences With Professional Care

### *Parenting a Parent Who Can No Longer Live Independently*

Many of our seniors will be blessed to live out their years wherever they choose—mobile, independent, and capable of self-care to the end. Some will not be so fortunate and will eventually need professional long-term care. Some will begin by downsizing from the family home to independent apartments for as long as their energy and mobility allow. They may then move on to assisted living, often in the same complex, then to the nursing home wing when greater care is indicated.

The multifaceted housing design is one good option, and excellent new facilities emerge yearly. Such innovative complexes allow seniors to continue to manage their own lives for a very long time. Respect and dignity, pride and independence, safety and security, and old-fashioned personal control are retained.

Some families will insist on their elders joining them in their homes to live out their final years. Others will reluctantly bring a parent into the home because it is the best option available, or even the only one.

In my own family's situation, none of those options were available for our dad. He was released from the hospital to a nursing home/sub acute rehabilitation center to strengthen bones and learn to walk again. He could not be released from there for a year, until a blood infection had healed sufficiently. Because of his long stay, Dad was in a sense both a short-term rehabilitation "patient" and a resident.

Dad's new home was a specialized setting near Jim and Jeanne's families. He had a semi-private room on the rehabilitation wing, with rotating roommates too numerous to count. They would come for rehab to strengthen a broken bone and return home after a month well on the way to recovery. Some had family who visited. Some did not. Some were friendly. Some were not. The room itself felt like a hospital, though the facility overall was filled with many options for live entertainment, a library, activities, and games.

Occasionally, Dad and other rehab patients pressed their call buttons and lay waiting for a response for a long time. Sometimes, my sister complained to the managers. When she found dad lying uncovered and undressed at noon she was appalled. Respect his dignity, she demanded. When both of dad's portable urinals were full but not emptied by staff, she was embarrassed for him. When dad said he'd pressed the call button two hours prior, she was outraged. When she observed someone literally throw dad back into the bed, she took it to the top. Such mishaps probably happen everywhere.

In physical therapy (PT) the staff was professionally trained, motivational, and supportive. Most of them did their jobs well. Dad was scheduled weekday mornings and afternoons for exercise to strengthen his upper and lower body. The PT staff knew us all by name, invited us to observe dad's exercise program, and reported his progress. They urged us to encourage him to walk more on his own, convinced that dad really could walk if he wanted to. In PT, the rehab patients cheered each other on. When a milestone was achieved, they clapped and shouted "Bravo!" When dad was cheered, he'd grin like a kid who had made an A on a paper. Praise is such a powerful motivator, no matter what age.

My siblings could stop by for a quick visit several times a week. But because I lived in Virginia and could only make it once a month to New Jersey, my visits had to be longer and more concentrated. At first, they were 9-12 hour marathons over several consecutive days, but I realized that while I had no trouble being with dad, wheeling him around, or finding ways to make him comfortable, I was inundated with sickness and death at every turn. I got depressed and grieved for all the patients and residents.

One night I returned to Jim's home, where I started to shake and cry upon entering. I proclaimed that I was never returning to the nursing home . . . ever! My family listened kindly to me and understood better than I did that I'd surpassed my inner endurance period for caregiving of that nature. Apparently, everyone has her own personal endurance—mine was seven hours. After that night, I decided to limit myself to those seven hours. Dad didn't like the idea—he'd want us to stay with him during all his waking hours if we could bear it—but I knew it was the right thing to do.

Overall, I enjoyed my monthly visits with my father. I met some extraordinary people on each visit: some I'd chat with while lounging in the day room, others would be working hard in the rehab center, and still others welcomed conversation in the dining room. I was impressed with the positive attitudes that bolstered them during their stay.

On Sunday mornings, religious services were conducted in the day room. Dad wheeled himself to his spot at 10 a.m. along with others. He smiled broadly when I volunteered to come early and attend church with him. A chair was waiting for me next to dad when I arrived. He introduced me to several people around him. Just like in church, everyone was sitting in regular seats. When the priest arrived, dad took his arm and introduced me. Such a touching gesture! It was Dad's home, Dad's priest, and Dad had someone to introduce to him. I brushed away my tears, and I looked around. Some had family present. Most did not.

On each of my visits to Dad, as I looked around and met some of the long-term residents, I observed a large number whose families never visited. One person received a birthday present, and then a Christmas present, through UPS . . . but no visit. Another's daughter visited once a year and called a couple of times in-between. Once, I overheard two fights between family members and the patient next to dad. The daughter's verbal outcries sounded cruel. Clearly, her dad was frightened by her rage.

On the days Dad and I ate in the dining room, I heard other stories of angry family members. Once, I overheard a conversation between a mom and her daughter. Mom wanted the daughter to come by every day. The daughter tried to tell her this was not possible. She worked full time and her family had needs, too. Mom didn't understand. She cried, feeling unloved and wounded by her daughter. The daughter cried in response. "I can't win, mom. I'm doing my best, and it's never good enough for you."

I understood both sides of the story. How lonely it must have been for the mother to endure so many days and nights in the nursing home, not free to come and go, not healthy enough to enjoy visiting others. Who else could she turn to but her daughter? How frustrating it was for the daughter, trying to do the right thing, sacrificing at home, taking the burdens on herself, compromising her own sleep to be with her mom as often as possible. Each had needs the other couldn't satisfy.

Nursing homes serve a valuable purpose. Living longer on earth changes all our expectations about the future. If we cannot manage life independently, then a nice home away from home is in order. Yet, when we are old and much of life is behind us, it must be a strange ending to our full lives, an ending with its share of "empty" moments.

One woman told me that she was not as lonely as I might think. She had learned to accept her aging, was appreciative of the care she received, the roof over her head, and the kind touch of someone each day. Her roommate chimed in: "If someone is interested in me, I'll gladly share my stories. I love telling them; it makes the memory sweeter! If not, my walker and I shuffle along."

For those alienated from their families, many stories can unfold. As long as family members are alive, hope for reconciliation or at least forgiveness exists. Aging can be a very complicated family affair.

Below are three poignant stories about women trying to make sense of the cards life dealt them.

## After the Fall

My friend Sue related the story of her Great Aunt Jane, who became important to her as Jane aged and needed care. Jane was aunt to Sue's dad. After World War II, Jane's marriage fell apart, leaving her to raise two children alone. When the kids grew up, they had infrequent contact with their mother, for reasons unknown. Their visits were brief, and usually only twice a year even though they lived less than two hours away. Jane lived independently most of her adult life near Sue's family. Sue remembers "Aunt Jane" being a regular in their home for Sunday dinners and holidays. Her parents looked after her needs.

When Sue's parents died, Sue became Aunt Jane's local caregiver by default, overseeing her grocery shopping, doctor visits, and occasional housekeeping tasks. This was not a burden for Sue. She rather liked this spunky 80-year-young person who was determined to live independently despite a serious handicap. Aunt Jane had suffered with macular degeneration for over a decade and was considered legally blind. Still, she managed her own life well enough . . . until the day she fell in the shower, where she lay unable to move for over 24 hours. It was there that Sue found her. (Today, Aunt Jane would be able to wear a call button, even in the shower, that would alert health care professionals to her plight, and help would be on the way within minutes.)

Aunt Jane spent a month in a hospital trying to heal a serious abrasion on her back, the only physical consequence of the fall. She would never fully recover, but when she was healthy enough, she was sent to the only local nursing home with an opening for a Medicaid patient. This was Aunt Jane's sole experience with a professional care facility. Staffing was limited, visits from her children became even more limited, and she never regained her feisty spirit. When her children did come to town, they assured their mom that she should stay in the nursing home—the care was just fine. Jane begged to go home, longing for the safety of her private and familiar space. The children's wishes prevailed.

Sue's recollection of Aunt Jane's time in the nursing home is a sad one. Sue remembers that floor caregivers were few and overworked. Aunt Jane often waited hours for help to the bathroom or even to have her sheets changed or her teeth brushed. She just wanted to go home. Not being her next of kin or having any legal standing, Sue was powerless to make that happen and was not free to confront the staff on her aunt's behalf. Aunt Jane died without ever going home again, barely six months after she first went to the nursing home. Her children came to the funeral that Sue organized and facilitated in her own church.

## Points to Ponder

Sue is this story's unsung hero. She was an observer to her aunt's plight with no legal power to facilitate changes on her behalf. Yet, she could, and did, make a difference in Jane's life. She brought a friendly presence, comfort, an interested ear, and early on, even groceries. This may be all that many of us in Sue's position can offer. Yet, the value of such gifts to the elderly on our paths is enormous. If you know someone like Aunt Jane with whom you occasionally visit and for whom you perform a few of life's basic tasks, then they are blessed to know you.

Spending time with those who are old, sick, slow of speech and hearing, living in less than adequate circumstances, and sometimes exuding aromas that are not always easy on the nose can be off-putting for the young, healthy, and oh-so-busy among us on life's fast track. So what? These people have feelings, needs, and life in their bones until the end. They have histories worth hearing, and points of view about today's world that are profound. Perhaps if we slow down to rest in their company awhile, we might *see* them. Such sharing brings mutual gifts that are life-sustaining.

## Dealing with Guilt: "Please Tell Me It's Not My Fault"

Linda's mom lived about twenty miles away in the city. Her mental faculties were failing, and the doctors called on Linda regularly, reporting worrisome incidents. Linda, a former client of mine and her mom's next of kin, was their point of contact. On one occasion, Linda's mother had gotten lost while driving, and a police officer had helped her return home. Another time, she knocked on her neighbor's door in the middle of the night in her pajamas to have a cup of tea. The neighbor called Linda to take her mom home. Most recently, her mom forgot to take her medications for almost a week. She collapsed in her front yard and was rushed to the emergency room after another neighbor saw her lying on the ground.

These problems and her mom's increasing memory loss could no longer be ignored. Even though Linda and her mom rarely got along, the doctor's call brought Linda into the center of her mother's choices. The time to intervene had arrived. Several doctors were consulted, tests were conducted, and medications were prescribed to forestall the progression of Alzheimer's disease. Linda talked with her mom more frequently and asked her to consider living with the family for her own safety. Her mom was adamant. "No! I don't want to live with you . . . ever. You won't take care of me well. I'm not leaving my home." Somehow, in her mental deterioration, she regarded Linda as dangerous. She was afraid of her own daughter, and nothing that anyone said could alleviate her fear. Fortunately, a power of attorney transfer had been successfully completed after the incident with the neighbor. Linda was in charge of bills and health care decisions. She talked with the doctors regularly.

"What would you like to do?" the doctor asked Linda, shortly after her mom's collapse. Linda's mother could no longer live alone. The choices were two: Linda could bring her into her home or find a suitable nursing home nearby. The doctor was kind, recommended several establishments, and said goodbye.

The decision was not easy for Linda. She was angry at her mother, a pent-up decades-long anger. Her mom, self-centered all her days, had put her daughter down in front of friends, criticized her many simple life choices, and blamed Linda for any inconveniences her mom may have experienced. So Linda felt guilt as well . . . was her mom right? Was she really the cause of her mother's problems? Could she trust her own reality, or should she apologize to her mom every time mom complained?

Such was the background for Linda and her wise and protective husband as they weighed their decisions. He was adamant that the nursing home option was the best choice for everyone. Considering the progression of the disease, such a place with a secured unit would be the safest setting. Linda's mom, however, was not happy to have been placed in a nursing home without her consent. She let everyone know it. She still wanted to go home.

Linda came to me for consultation. What could she do? She felt guilty; her mom's despondency pierced her like a knife because she continued relentlessly to blame Linda for her current situation. For the longest time, her mother's criticism extended to Linda's choice in friends, even her style of clothing and hair. More than ever, now that her mom was sick and fragile, Linda yearned to be appreciated by her mother with whatever parts of her brain that still connected to the truth.

"Please tell me it's not my fault," she cried in my office. I reminded her that no one else's words would free her from her guilt. She would know what to do if she listened to her heart. Unfortunately, my voice trailed in the wind. Linda was not healing—and she would not heal as long as she relied on my wisdom on this issue. She needed to claim the truth within her: she is not to blame for her mother's unhappiness.

## Points to Ponder

Three issues stand out here. First, Linda and her mom have been entangled for decades. Mom, myopic, enmeshed, and self-focused in her understanding of her daughter, devalued Linda for many of her personal choices. Healthy people would see how ridiculous and childish such cutting remarks are. But Linda's identity has been connected to her mother's in such a destructive manner that Linda could not find a way to begin to separate her "self" from the way her mom sees her. I have never met Linda's mom, but it's possible that she, too, was not supported on her own womanly journey as a child and thus never found her own center. She may well be trying to live her life through her daughter. It seems she would invade Linda's friendships and court her friends, who loved having "fun" mom around. Whenever this occurred, Linda retreated into the shadows. Today, Linda, the child of an intrusive parent, must break from the power her mother has over her, claim her own life, and risk the separation that might set her free.

Linda's self-perceived inadequacy has defined her most of her life. Despite years of counseling, Linda continues to struggle with what we call neurotic guilt. Is she guilty for her mom's state of unrest? Of course not! Is the mom right when labeling Linda? Of course not! What should Linda do?

Whatever her gut instincts tell her to do! Who will tell Linda the right thing to do with and for her mom? Probably no one has the "right answer" for her mother's situation, because there isn't one. Linda must follow her own heart and do what seems the best for her.

This inner turmoil is problematic in and of itself in a daughter who is in her 40s, but it is even more challenging when her mother's disease is such that she doesn't remember from hour to hour what she's just said to hurt Linda's feelings. As the only caregiver, Linda feels compelled to visit her mom, while she strives to keep hold of her inner boundaries. Thankfully, Linda is beginning to take specific steps to strengthen her newfound self. She limits the number and length of her visits with her husband's help. In the past, if Linda stayed around long enough to take it, her mother would bombard her with criticisms and demands. Those days are over.

"Please tell me it's not my fault" is a plea that no one can answer for Linda. She must come to terms with the situation and make her decisions as best she can. When her mom tells the nursing home staff that Linda is keeping her prisoner there and (among other things) stealing her perfume, Linda should take a deep breath and remain quiet. She doesn't need to defend herself. Of course, mom's accusations are absurd! She has the practical voice of a husband to steady her, and she has come to count on the wisdom of the nursing home staff, who deal with these sorts of accusations every day. They know well the emotional turmoil that children of disturbed parents endure.

Linda is trying to think rationally. Mom's power in Linda's life, the power that the daughter allowed her mom to wield, has consumed Linda. Now it is Linda's turn to use her authority as respectfully as she can to set very clear limits. When her mother demands that Linda come right over (an hour's drive), Linda now says "no, I have prior plans. I'll see you tomorrow." If her mom demands lobster bisque or apple pie on the way to or from a doctor's appointment, Linda tells her there is no time in the schedule to stop for these specialties. Perhaps next time they can plan a restaurant stop.

The more Linda speaks up with self-care as her goal, the less guilty she feels and the more reality she grasps. Peace has begun to untangle her knotted heart. These days, her mom is agitated because she's no longer getting her own way. Perhaps, the only consolation is that she forgets her requests shortly after she makes them! Linda still visits regularly but takes her mother's demands and devaluings much less seriously.

The third issue encompasses the others. Parenting a parent who doesn't want to be parented is difficult in any circumstances. As noted in earlier chapters, if the adult children don't enter their elders' worlds respectfully early on, entering with authority when the parent's health is compromised will be problematic.

Increasingly in recent years, I am hearing more stories that bear fruit due to honest communication by a parent's bedside in a nursing home. Controversial topics can be initiated and continue over several visits. After a lifetime of misunderstanding, time to reflect on each other's assumptions, conclusions, and interpretations can be a good thing. "I thought you thought . . . " and "I never intended to convey . . . " can free burdened families if they give each other the opportunity.

Still, early intervention is advisable. Engage the family lovingly early on, before accidents or old age mandate interventions. Plan ahead for the unexpected, and gain permission for different decisions that, at the time of execution, may be hated by the parent. At the very least, create a written document reflecting the parent's desires for the adult children to follow. Guilt will have no doorway. Only sadness and weariness can enter . . . and everyone will find those understandable.

## When One Aging Parent Cares for Another: "If You Won't Go to the Nursing Home, I Must."

Millie and Joe were married for almost 50 years. Joe was a tough guy. Ever a loner, he rarely allowed Millie to host a dinner party or create other family or friend gatherings. Outside of work, he counted on no one except Millie. He always assumed that Millie would cater to all his needs. For five years Joe had been relegated to a wheelchair in their home and was bitter about his limited mobility. Perhaps Joe took his anger out on Millie, whose legs worked just fine. He asked her to use them a lot.

Millie, a former client, followed a traditional script and waited on her husband hand and foot. She hoped Joe would appreciate her efforts, but he never did. He rarely said "thank you" and never praised her. He didn't share feelings of love, fear, or any other sentiments, except anger. He barked orders and then counted on Millie to be his companion and watch a movie with him every night.

One afternoon, Millie fainted in their living room. Joe wheeled himself over to the phone, dialing 911 with shaky hands. Millie was rushed to the emergency room. Within a couple of days she was sent to a nursing home, medicated, and informed that she had almost killed herself from exhaustion and lack of self-care. Too often on the receiving end of Joe's tirades, Millie had experienced a physical and mental breakdown. She had lost her grip on reality and began talking nonsense. It took the better part of nine months, but with time, rest, and proper medications, she regained her senses and re-energized her body. Millie had recovered enough to return home.

During the time of Millie's stay in the nursing home, Joe needed care. Because he refused to leave home, in-home help was ordered. Someone stayed with him overnight, cooked his meals, and helped him bathe and dress, He was taught to be more active and self-responsible despite his wheelchair. He and Millie talked occasionally, but Millie was given strict instructions not to put herself in upsetting situations, and talking with Joe was often an upsetting situation. With each phone call, oblivious to his wife's pressing needs, he asked when she was coming home to take care of him, noting that the caregivers didn't pay enough attention to him. With coaching from a social worker on staff, Millie limited her calls to once a week.

I met again with Millie when she left the nursing home. She was a changed woman. She had found her voice at age 75. Through therapy, she'd learned that she couldn't do it all on her own. She had to say "no" and mean it. She was to limit herself to what she felt capable of doing. My role now was to reinforce the goals she'd set for herself when she returned home. We reviewed new ways of talking with Joe. Millie was highly apprehensive about confronting Joe with any of her needs, but she knew that she'd be back in the nursing home if she didn't speak up.

Millie came to the second session all smiles. "I told Joe that I get anxious when he raises his voice to me. I asked him not to do it. He said he didn't think he raised his voice at all, made a nasty face at me, and wheeled himself into another room. I felt awful and stayed away from him all afternoon. At dinner, Joe told me that he didn't want me to get sick and go away again. He said he missed me when I was in the nursing home. He promised to stop talking loud. I asked him if I could tell him when he was sounding angry at me, and he agreed." Millie reported this conversation like a kid who had just passed a big test in school. She no longer showed signs of the stress that broke her down. Joe was still demanding . . . and loud. But he was trying, in his own fashion, not to upset her too much.

Eight months later, Joe died. Millie felt a little guilty that she had abdicated her "job" to care for him. She wondered if she'd hastened his death by getting sick and not being there for him. I asked her if she really thought that was true. "I learned in the nursing home that Joe's situation and his unhappiness with life were not my fault. I do believe this is true today. Still, every now and again, I question if I could have done more."

## Points to Ponder

Millie was born in 1932. She was taught from childhood how to be a good wife—"take care of a husband's every need." Millie tried all her life to care for Joe the way that her mom had looked after Millie's dad. The problem was that Joe was not like her dad, an independent man who enjoyed doing many things on his own. Joe was the kind of guy who expected to be catered to. And Millie was the perfect partner for his belief system.

As Millie matured, she knew this wasn't right, and she began to want more from life. She wanted to make her own decisions . . . but each time she stepped out of character and did so, she paid a high price for her efforts by incurring her husband's wrath. When Joe got sick, Millie worked even harder to please him. His slow deterioration and rather empty life kept him increasingly focused on Millie. He was angry at God, at his weakened body, at his unfinished life, and of course, he took it all out on unsuspecting, compliant Millie, until she collapsed.

The nine months in a nursing home changed Millie's life forever. She was 75, but her life wasn't over. She took notes in therapy sessions, read books, and began to speak her mind with Joe. Despite his often negative reactions, Millie thrived. Then, Joe died and Millie continued to flourish . . . except when she entertained the thought that she was responsible for his death. On those days, depression would wrap itself around her for a few hours. After a while, though, she'd remember that she was not liable for Joe's life choices or his time of death. She'd call her sister to have dinner, and the depression would dissipate.

Millie has adapted to single life very well. She is at peace, most of the time, and enjoys her friends, sisters, and church associates. She has chosen for now to remain in the home she and Joe shared together. She has had the family room, where Joe spent the majority of his days, painted and redecorated. She's most excited by the new sofa she bought, and she giggled like a child when she told me about it. Then Millie dug in her purse for a photograph. I expected to see a picture of the sofa, but it was of a cat. She had purchased a kitten to keep her company.

Traditional, modern, or unconventional—the roles we take in marriage should never include emotional abuse by a partner. On the one hand, it's sad that it took Millie half a century to find her voice. On the other hand, she found it! Some, unfortunately, never do.

Childlike fear had stifled Millie's self-assertion for a long time. What she failed to notice was that Joe needed her more than she needed him. He wasn't going to leave her. If she had been able to capture this truth early on, she may have risked speaking her mind sooner.

I'd like to add that if some couples do divorce because one partner breaks old molds and develops self-care, those marriages did not have the necessary roots to sustain them. If speaking up for oneself and asserting boundaries does end a marriage, then it was going to end at some point anyway. This was not going to happen to Millie and Joe. Unfortunately, it would take Millie a long time to realize this truth.

Doing the right thing is unique to each family. Yet, often we can benefit from choices others have made on the journey. How do we choose where our loved ones will spend their last years? How do others tackle this choice?

# 5

# Where Will Dad (Or Mom) Live?
## Knowing Our Caregiving Strengths and Limitations

Sooner or later, almost all of us face the question of where our parent(s) will live. In the case of my own family, this question arose after my father "graduated" from the rehab center where he had been staying. He needed a home. Time to live out his life . . . somewhere. His early need for professional care had to some degree taken the need for decision-making out of our hands. As taxing as the year had been, we realized in retrospect that it was a piece of cake compared to what lay ahead for us as a family.

Even more so than before, it was time for us to face our individual biases and strengths. We assessed our own needs and those of our sub-families. We reconsidered the ramifications of a long-term commitment to house dad in one of our homes because we knew that was what dad wanted. My siblings and I had tentatively discussed where dad would live after his nursing home stay, but the amount of attention that he would continue to need for the rest of his life rendered our previous thoughts inadequate.

"Who will I live with?" he asked me during one of my visits to the nursing home that summer, when it was suggested he might be ready to leave in the fall. "Who will I live with?" he asked Jeanne. "Who will I live with?" he asked John and Jim. "Who will he live with?" we asked each other for the hundredth time.

We now knew that dad would never again walk well enough to live on his own, let alone climb the stairs to his bedroom in his house on Long Island, and that he'd need handicap access. We knew that even if he could walk, he'd forget to take his medications or, forgetting he'd already taken them, overdose on them. We understood that dad needed to live in a safe setting where someone oversaw his care all day long. None of us could make that happen without professional help.

All for legitimate reasons, none of my local siblings could envision dad living with them—even with professional help. Jobs, space limitations, a spouse's needs, young children to care for, were all considerations. Like my siblings, I tried on the notion of bringing dad to my home. Could I care for him? Should I? Would dad be isolated in Virginia from the rest of the family hundreds of miles away?

"I must tell dad my truth," I reminded myself. One day, after dodging his questions several times, I outlined, in as casual a manner as I could muster, the obstacles he'd encounter at any of the local homes. He never said a word, and he never lost eye contact. It was a candid and painful one-way conversation. "So I can't have you come live with me, Dad," I finally said, clearly and definitively. Dad held my gaze but still said nothing. It broke my heart.

"Who will I live with?" Dad asked Jeanne later that week while sitting in his wheelchair in the garden of the nursing home. My sister's home had no handicap access, no "extra" room, and she was already busy fulltime with her family's needs. There were too many steps to climb; they'd need to build a separate room for him, which would be costly. Jeanne braced herself and then, she, too, told dad that her home would not work for him.

Dad was sad. Surely, he must have thought, one of his six children would take care of him when he left the rehab center. Each of our brothers told dad that they were considering all options, including local assisted-living centers. Still, dad remained silent.

Our local explorations bore fruit. Much to our surprise, the best option was right under our noses. A new branch of a national senior assisted-living chain was under construction 200 yards from my sister's house. We visited one of the existing facilities in the next town to check it out, and we loved it.

Sometime before fall, Bill and Fred came east for two weeks. Their visit again positioned Bill to be the family spokesperson. He told Dad that the assisted-living centers Dad knew we'd been investigating were now option #1. "Would you be willing to visit one with us?" Bill asked. Later that day, Bill and Fred escorted Dad to the car, wheelchair in tow, to tour our model facility in the next town.

Dad never again asked where he'd live. He understood his situation and kept his own counsel. When he did speak, it was to select the specific apartment that would suit him.

Your own family's deliberations over housing choices for your parents may in some ways resemble those of my own family. Caring for your parents is part of life's requirements. People like your parents are not disposable simply because they may be old, incapacitated, and needy, or because their children still have "issues" with them. Here are several stories that might help you develop better Family Speak with your parents and with others involved in the decision making process.

## The Challenges of Living under the Same Roof: Whose House Is This, Anyway?

For Margie, a current client age 60, the question of where her father would live, after her mom died, had only one answer. He would stay put in his current house, and she would move in. She sold her apartment in New York City, put her belongings in storage, and moved in with her dad in Virginia. Margie was his last surviving family member; Dad was 87 and somewhat fragile. He hadn't driven a car in several years, didn't cook for himself, was forgetful, and not surprisingly, was still grieving the loss of his wife of over 65 years. Margie was newly divorced and free to make changes to her life. She opted for early retirement from work. Even though they'd never been particularly close, it was the right thing for her to do.

One afternoon, almost two years into their shared living arrangement, Margie stomped into my office letting out steam. Her father was driving her crazy. That morning, after a storm, she'd asked his opinion on some structural damage to the chimney and while talking to him inadvertently stepped on the carpet in front of the fireplace. Her father had yelled at her to get off. Why? Because, she explained, he and her mom had never walked on that carpet. They had instructed the housekeeper to vacuum in such a way that it would never look walked on! In her anxiety over the safety of the house, Margie had forgotten this particular rule, and instead of being grateful to her, her father was yelling. So Margie yelled back, demanding that her father get up and inspect the chimney. He maneuvered himself so that he only touched a corner of the rug. Margie was fuming. This was so typical of her dad, who was unwilling for her to rearrange furniture, remove any of her mother's treasures, or even buy a new sofa. When he left the room, she stomped all over the carpet, while laughing somewhat ruefully at herself knowing that she was acting like a rebellious kid.

On another occasion, Margie decided to buy something special for dinner. She spent over $20 on grouper and fixings, set a pretty table with cloth napkins, and even lit a candle. Her father looked at the fish and took one bite. "What's the matter?" Margie asked. "Nothing," he said. "Come on, Dad," she insisted. Finally, he told her that he didn't like grouper and that her mother would have known. Although he didn't say so, his response reflected all that he felt was wrong with his life: he missed his wife, he was growing older and losing his faculties, and he resented being dependent on his daughter and no longer in control of his own life. His daughter, for her part, felt defeated.

It had been two years since Margie had moved in with her dad. After that length of time, she could no longer live comfortably as a guest in someone else's home. Her dad's house was hers to manage, but it was not her home. She was in a no-win situation, with most of the responsibility but little authority. Worse, despite moments when she and her father did get along, their togetherness was crowding her. If she thought of taking a vacation, a nagging guilt and her father's don't-leave-me expression kept her from doing so. Instead, she filled her days with activities and tried to get out of the house more often. However, her distress returned every time she pulled into the driveway.

## Points to Ponder

Margie's story echoes many that I've heard over the past few years. Before my dad's own life changes, I might not have heard her well. I might even have placated her a little, judged her as being childish and selfish, and thought she should be more generous with her dad. My focus would have been primarily on her dad's loss. Not anymore! Transitions for *all* involved are disquieting in every family. How those involved deal with change depends on the day, their differing needs, and their ability, or lack of ability, to adapt to other changes on the horizon.

Several issues surface with Margie's story. First, Margie's dad had lost his partner and confidant of many decades; he was very lonely, and life would never be the same for him again. He was disconnected from his local colleagues and was trying to find new connections through his daughter. This didn't make up for his losses, and he knew it, but it was all he could do. Death would call him one day. But death was not knocking today. He deserved much compassion for his plight.

Second, Margie has lost as well. She has lost her mom; she's retired from her job, no longer enjoys direct access to her friends and home, and has moved out of her comfort zone to care for her dad, with whom she was never close. Some days, his confusion over Margie's role in his life, and his intrusion into what little space she can call her own, are enough to drive her crazy. She, too, deserves compassion for the generosity of spirit that guides her caregiving role.

Third, sharing space with her invalid dad would take its toll on anyone after a couple of years, even if he were younger and his faculties intact. Around the two-year mark, many of us lose the ability to live comfortably as a guest in someone else's home; it's as though an unconscious trigger has been set off. Margie's annoyances at her dad's ways are a reflection of this phenomenon. She feels an urgency to make the home more her own, even if she's not sure she will want to live there after her dad dies. She's currently in a bind. The home is hers to manage but not her home to redesign in any way. To remain sane, Margie needs to acknowledge this dual reality and tension in her life. At least she can validate her frustration if not resolve it. It's real and understandable. It has an end, even if not in the visible future.

Fourth, Margie's peace cannot be in her dad's hands or dependent on his fluctuating moods. For example, she would benefit from cooking what she might enjoy and, if he chooses, letting dad pick at his food or not eat it at all. I suspect that her dad is not focused on food much at this time anyway. As with many people in his situation, he may not even take pleasure in what has traditionally been his favorite dinner.

Fifth, living with each other is a new experience for both Margie and her dad. Neither of them knows how to manage their shared life gracefully. Dad doesn't know how to act differently, and she doesn't know how to receive his ways kindly. Holding in emotions and stomping on rugs is a momentary release, but regular candid conversations would help them both with long-term solutions. To their credit, after several months of frequent discussions, Margie and her dad are now better adapted to each other, even if these discussions are sometimes confrontational in nature.

Lastly, the difficult fact is that Margie lives with an elderly, fragile man, whose health is questionable. She works hard to set aside her ongoing fear of his death and what might be required of her at that time. Yet, this fear lies below the surface every day. The anticipation, and dread, of dad's passing is bound to take a toll on her from time to time! Of course, it must take a toll on her dad, too. He seems less psychologically and verbally skilled than Margie, so he may not be as articulate about what he is experiencing, but he is no less afraid and overwhelmed. Even so, they both acknowledge that the arrangement is good enough for them. They choose the life that is offered to them today.

"Where will mom or dad live?" is a powerful question with life-changing ramifications. Scenes like the one described above are not limited to in-home caregiving. They happen regularly when we are caregivers for our parents, even if we have our own separate space and visit them often at a nursing home or senior living center. Our parents' worlds are shrinking, and their defense against this reality can make us feel as if we are being consumed. It seems that we can never do enough, stay long enough, or do whatever we do well enough. Stepping back from these feelings for a bit can help us restore our sense of reality, return us to our world of choices, and free us to appreciate the opportunities during these times.

## Determined to Do It Alone

Phil and Karen, a former client, live in Florida. Phil's 90-year-old parents live in Georgia, about an eight-hour drive away. Phil's brother lives about four hours from his parents in South Carolina. Both brothers are non-confronters and non-decision makers. This was not an issue until their parents started a rapid physical and mental decline about two years ago. Their dad's aging brought about various illnesses that now limit his mobility and require a lot of his attention. Their mom's decade-long partial paralysis requires frequent medical help. Her increasing forgetfulness has started more than one fire in the kitchen. Until a year ago, this couple was fully opposed to any outside help.

Karen grew increasingly disquieted during one of her bi-monthly trips with her husband to visit his parents.

Karen's mother-in-law told Karen that she and her husband wanted to die together. Karen was sure this meant that they intended to stay in their home till death claimed them—no matter if they forgot to take pills or if the house caught fire. They weren't leaving. Karen reported this discussion to Phil, who, for a while, seemed to dismiss Karen's concerns.

Finally, Karen said: "Phil, your mom and dad really need meals on wheels, someone to clean their home, and definitely a caregiver to help your mom bathe." Phil panicked. "I can't tell Mom and Dad that!"

During each visit to her in-laws' home, Karen anticipated with anxiety the mess that would greet her, often spending the better part of those visits cleaning and cooking meals to store in the refrigerator. Phil helped, but he continued to turn a deaf ear to her warnings.

Karen didn't want to be intrusive or disrespect her husband, but on one occasion she could not leave Georgia without talking with Phil's parents. As painful as it was for her to do so, if they died in their house because she had decided to say nothing, she would never forgive herself. Karen prepared Phil for the talk ahead.

Phil's mom and dad were highly offended by Karen when she mentioned the subject. They told Karen that it was none of her business, and if she was not willing to accept their ways, she didn't have to visit anymore. Karen wasn't intimidated, and now that the ice was broken, she wouldn't be stopped. The danger at hand fueled her heartfelt intervention. She was on a roll.

Karen told her in-laws that she was contacting meals on wheels to deliver hot, healthy dinners each day. She told them that their sons were going to hire a caregiver to help Mom three days a week for three hours each visit. After inquiring with Medicare, Karen also informed them that a nurse would be checking in on both of them twice a week. Dad told Karen that she could do whatever she wanted, but he would not let anyone in. Karen looked at Phil. Phil looked at the floor. The irrationality was escalating. Karen and Phil returned to Florida after lunch.

On the way home, Phil thanked Karen for taking charge. "I'm afraid for them now, too, Karen. We can't let them stay there, and it's clear that they will not leave of their own accord. Yet, I can't be the one to make them leave." Karen suggested that the brothers should alert the medical community to the seriousness of the problem. It was more than time for a doctor to declare both of them incompetent. Phil agreed.

The father and mother did let the helpers in. One afternoon two months later, while the caregiver was bathing mom, dad collapsed on the living room floor. An ambulance rushed him to the hospital, and both brothers drove long distances to help out. Apparently, their father had not taken his medications for several days. Health care professionals were called in, and a nursing home with two available beds was found. They were each declared incompetent and incapable of ever living on their own again.

## Points to Ponder

This is a sad story on two fronts. First, the elderly couple is legally within their rights to live in their home for as long as they choose, within certain health parameters. At the same time, the pact they made to die together has endangered them and is unacceptable. Social services and the medical community have been forced to intervene.

Second, the brothers seem unreasonably powerless at this stage of their lives. Karen's more objective eyes and outspoken manner nudged the family to the proper place. The heartbreaking part of the story centers on the lack of any productive Family Speak. The children in this family were never received as grown-ups. They faced angry parental judgment whenever they tried to intervene. They remained children to in-charge parents, no matter how not-in-charge the parents were. They had no history of speaking frankly with their parents and remained terrified. Although fully aware of their caregiving limitations, they were abandoning elderly parents to their meager mental and physical resources. This is never the answer.

In a situation like this, I would definitely recommend therapy for both brothers. Such fear of speaking the truth is dangerous for their parents and quite likely permeates and weakens other aspects of their lives as well.

How would we handle such a situation in our own families? Perhaps we tell ourselves that we'd never let conditions deteriorate to that level. And we might be right. But some of us will feel fear in the pit of our gut and avoid the dreaded conversations for as long as possible.

The question about where aging parents should live when they can no longer be independent will continue to emerge in all households. The corollary question of who decides *when* the parents' independence must end remains ambiguous. The answers are not always obvious and rarely simple.

## In-Town Caregivers

Sandy is a colleague and fellow clinician. She and her husband Bob have answered the question "Where will they live?" in a unique manner. Sandy and Bob are in their 60s; he's a retired family doctor and she, a full-time psychologist. They reside within a mile of their elderly families, who live independently. Bob's mom is 94 and lives in her home of many years with her daughter, age 53, who has Down's Syndrome. Bob shops for them, visits several times a week, and drives his mom around town. She looks forward to these outings and makes sure that Bob knows in advance where she wants to go on any given day, so that he'll allow enough time.

Sandy's mom is 86 and her dad is 90. They live 13 miles away with Sandy's brother, who is brain-injured and a diagnosed schizophrenic. Her brother recently had a heart attack. Her mom and dad have each survived cancer episodes. Even so, Sandy's parents are high functioning. Dad still drives. Bob sees that their needs are tended to during the week as well. Sandy talks with her parents two times a day, on the way to work and on the way home from work. All the parents and handicapped siblings come to Sandy and Bob's home on Sundays for dinner. "Our parents come first," Sandy told me. "We wouldn't have it any other way. There are no questions and no conflicts. We support each other fully."

When I asked her what fears she might have, her response was understandable. "Bob and I are both concerned about the sequence of events that are to come. Who will need care? Will all of them need care at the same time? We can't answer any of these questions. We can only be present to them and be prepared for whatever comes."

## Points to Ponder

It's rare these days that extended families live so near each other. It's even rarer when husband and wife are *so* connected, in tune to the needs of their elders, mutually respectful of "family," and open to adapting their lives for as long as God gives them the opportunity to care for their parents. Sunday dinners may become somewhat tiring, but love makes up for the weariness.

Love alone would not have brought this family to such a workable routine. One-on-one conversations with each parent, along with countless conversations between husband and wife, forged this path. The parents were grateful that their children would help them keep the status quo as long as possible, that is, live in their own settings. Bob and Sandy spent the six months prior to Bob's retirement going over all possible occurrences and then potential consequences for them as a couple. Goodness and acceptable routines emerged because they had been able to talk most of life's issues through with each other. Talking about caring for their less independent parents would be an easy extension of years of healthy communicating.

Even this goodness can turn south if Sandy and Bob don't take breaks from their caregiving. Dinners alone, weekends away, and other special couple times will help them sustain the pace. Without such breaks and the nurturing of each other, their good intentions may not survive, except in shorter and shorter increments.

Once living arrangements are decided, families work toward creating a satisfying experience for their loved ones.

Margie lives with her dad but must ensure that she find her own space. Karen and Phil have finally placed the caregiving responsibilities in the hands of professionals. Sandy and Bob support their parents' independence by supervising their activities themselves.

Doing the right thing is rarely, if ever, the result of simple formulas. Born out of deep complexities, each choice must be considered in order to find the best fit for the unique needs of each family.

# 6

## Doing the Right Thing (Whatever That Is)

### *From Prescribed Scripts to the Wisdom of the Heart*

Throughout the process of strengthening Family Speak, you and your family will identify several options for caregiving. How do you choose the "right" one? How do you know that your decisions were the best you could have made? Sometimes, you will only know in retrospect that your decisions were at least good enough.

My family's option for assisted living, for example, proved to be a great choice for Dad, who adapted well to his new environment. He moved into the new building early in 2006 with all levels of staff eager to please. Dad was a resident with his own apartment, no longer a patient with a roommate. He had a home again.

Dad's one-bedroom, second-floor apartment was spacious and attractive, with a large window overlooking one of the gardens, and we enjoyed visiting him there. Jeanne's family decorated his quarters, making the place cozy with special photos and family treasures. My brothers bought dad a 32" screen TV for viewing the sports he loved, and Jeanne filled the kitchen cabinets with glasses and drinks so that he could entertain properly. Dad set his phone, a drink, and his TV remote control next to the new blue recliner that we'd purchased. It fit perfectly into a corner of the living area. Settling into a routine, every morning after breakfast he read his paper in his recliner, and relaxed a little for the first time since Mom died.

Some of the spry lady residents were interested in our handsome dad. Once they found out he loved chocolate, they seized every opportunity to feed him. When they knew that doctors' appointments would cause him to miss meals, he'd often find a chocolate cupcake or cookie on his kitchen table upon his return. (Rarely did the residents lock their doors. Open doors allowed caregivers immediate access in case of emergency.) So, wheelchair-bound and 83 years old, he could still turn heads. More relaxed, and surrounded by people who cared about him, he had what he needed to thrive, in a setting that, under the circumstances, couldn't have been nicer. After several months of observing dad in this setting, we realized that we had done the right thing by choosing this home for him.

"Did we do the right thing?" We had to act on our inclinations and choose our best options long before we would know the answer to that question. Perhaps the same will occur for you. Two struggles are embedded in one choice: making the right decision for and with your loved ones; and surviving the uncertainty about whether you chose well (based on your loved one's lived-out response). Waiting for that positive response can eat away at even the most healthy adults.

My family had agonized over making the right decision for Dad's living arrangements. We took the situation step by step. Early on, we had hoped that we wouldn't have to hurt him by stating out loud that none of us could house him. Holding back discussions with our dad on future housing until necessary was understandable, and common to many families, but it is not the best way to approach the situation. It would have been better for us to have initiated the frank conversations earlier—although, by the time we did talk with Dad, he must have been resigned to the inevitable.

Early conversations with your parents about their care in extended Family Speak are a good beginning. The worst that can happen in any event is that folks will disagree. In that case, the option comes off the table. On to the next! If everyone's intentions are loving, then all comments are in service of reaching consensus.

The following stories illustrate that "doing the right thing" is rarely crystal clear from the outset.

## Too Much Help: "Don't Treat Me Like an Invalid!"

When I met Connie, her mother Tess was 80 years old. Connie and her husband, Steve, were planning to leave Milwaukee where they'd lived five miles from mom for 36 years. They had purchased a large piece of property in the country about 90 miles away and built their retirement home. Connie wanted to bring her mom with them, Tess didn't want to leave the city, and Steve was secretly apprehensive about bringing his mother-in-law into his home.

Connie and I talked regularly. Then, Steve asked to speak with me privately as well. In that conversation, he told me he was fearful his privacy would be compromised. Among other things, he was used to walking around the house in his underwear, and getting up in the middle of the night if he couldn't sleep to turn on the TV. I asked him if something else might be bugging him. "Well, it sounds silly," he replied, "but I'm afraid Connie will give more of her attention to her mom. I don't want to become a third wheel in my own home."

That's what was on his heart!

Steve wanted his wife to himself, and he wanted freedom to visit their three adult children and their little ones, who lived in different states. Who would care for his mother-in-law when they traveled?

It was time to meet Tess. To my surprise, she was eager to speak with me as well. Her concerns were many. First, Tess wanted to assure me that she was of sound mind and body, and was not old and fragile like others her age. She loved her life in the city and had no intention of moving to the country with Connie and Steve—not for many years to come.

Second, Tess had grown significantly independent during the ten years she'd lived alone, after her husband died. She worked at the community center with friends three days a week, played bridge often, and drove her friends to their doctors' appointments, as she was the only one still driving. Such independence, coupled with pride in her competence, would be surrendered only reluctantly. Tess was sure it was not her time to do so.

Third, several trips to visit Connie and Steve had convinced Tess that they saw her as an old lady who needed to rest, someone who should avoid chores and cooking and be satisfied with regular conversations on the many topics they all enjoyed discussing. Connie and Steve would take charge of the physical tasks. Tess reported to Connie that she would lose her sense of value and usefulness if she moved in with them now, but Connie seemed not to understand. So Tess became more explicit: "When I visit with you, I offer to cook, and you tell me to stay put. When I offer to assist Steve with a project, he tells me to relax; he'll take care of whatever task is at hand. When I offer to make dessert while you are busy preparing dinner, you seem offended that I even offer. I'm not ill; I can walk, drive, cook, and clean. I do so in my own home at will. Why do you think I should do otherwise when I'm with you?"

Connie was shocked by Tess's candor. She had no idea that her mom was so offended by what she had intended as respect. Connie apologized for misunderstanding her mom's needs and then spoke candidly herself: "I understand now why it's so important for you to stay in your own home. I won't fight you on your decision today. But promise me that if you become incapacitated for any reason, you'll come live with us—even if only for a few months. Promise me, also, that when you're much older and less able to care for yourself with ease, you'll agree to move to the country with us." Tess readily agreed.

I asked both of these women how it was that, despite their strong relationship and good communication skills, they had not been able to complete this heart-to-heart discussion by themselves. I find that it is not uncommon for families to create scenarios in their heads that have nothing to do with the reality of other family members—even in families that know each other fairly well and have strong relationships. So I wanted to hear them articulate aloud the conclusions they each formed about the other that blocked fruitful outcomes.

Connie admitted that she was probably at fault in their communication breakdown. In her desire to be a good daughter, she believed that she should not impose on her mom at all. Therefore, she rejected her mother's suggestions. On her part, Tess owned that she hadn't been forceful or clear in speaking up for herself. She would try to be more direct in the future.

As it turned out, Tess would spend ten more years in the city. When she neared 90, several of her friends and bridge partners died of natural causes within a year of each other, sending Tess into depression. She lost weight, retreated from her volunteer work, and rarely connected with the few friends she had left. She ended up in the emergency room and, ultimately, a month-long hospital stay. It was time for Connie to bring Tess to the country.

About this time, Connie learned of a new housing complex being built three miles from their home. She brought her mother to see the apartments, assuring her that her privacy and autonomy would be respected. The single-story units, organized as four-plexes, were edged with brightly-colored flowers. Tess nodded her approval and moved in. She recovered from her depression and enjoyed another ten years near Connie, remaining independent to the end.

Two birthday parties were planned for Tess when she turned 100. One was hosted by Connie and Steve—a huge multi-generational celebration. The whole family gathered together in one setting to honor Tess! It touched her deeply.

The second party was held at the senior center where Tess had volunteered until she was 96. (Connie had secured transportation back to the city for Tess once a month.) Five staff, two old friends, and twenty residents cheered as she entered the room. A few months later, Tess died peacefully in her sleep.

### Points to Ponder

The Tesses of the world are going to multiply. Many are 80 years young. They have local roots, good enough health, autonomy—and they don't want to be treated as if they are old or fragile. That said, how should their children respond? They, too, are carrying senior status; they've long since tired of the city and are hungering to retire in comfort. Doing the right thing is complicated sometimes.

The first issue is one of imposition. The healthy Tesses don't want someone else's plans for them superimposed on their lives. They want to be heard and deserve options, too. We must discard the notion that we have the single right plan for someone else to choose, making room for dialogue and allowing the uniqueness of each situation to call forth options.

A second issue opens up the sticky topic of the right each of us has to decide how to die. If Tess wants to take her risks in the city, who is Connie to tell her otherwise, even in the name of being a good daughter? It's Tess's life to design.

Of course, if Tess should develop dementia, or begin to drive erratically, or get sick due to a medication overdose . . . that's another story. Such happenings are red flags, raising the dilemma faced by Phil and Karen in the last section. In that case, it is definitely the family's job to step in, even against the senior's wishes. But Tess is of sound mind and must be honored for her realistic desires. She is near doctors, hospitals, friends, and church. It's Connie's job to let go and celebrate her mother's marvelous example.

The Connies of the world must distinguish practical reality from their own inner noise regarding "doing the right thing." If they can let go of their own *shoulds* (Mom should do what I think she should do, so that I can be a good daughter) and respect their parent's choices, the right time for change will become clear. If decisions are guided by shoulds, however, more tugs-of-war can be expected.

## Small Town—Family Support

Dorothy, my Uncle Fred's wife, was 69 when her husband of 45 years died suddenly, soon after treatment for a duodenal ulcer. One night, he lay down on the sofa after dinner for a nap and never woke up. Dorothy found him when she had finished washing the dishes and returned to the TV room with her cup of tea. He was 71. He was her whole world. He was her rock. He was gone.

Dorothy was overwhelmed and frightened. She called her sister, who lived in town. The sister called Dorothy's only son, Tom, to tell him his dad had died. Only 200 miles away, Tom and his wife packed up the family and drove to his mother's home early the next morning.

When the family arrived, they found Dorothy wandering around the house with her pajama top open, no slippers, no robe. It was the middle of winter. She didn't know where the insurance papers or other important documents were filed. She did remember the name of the family attorney, and her friend who owned the funeral home. This was a very small town. Word had spread fast, and before daybreak everyone had learned that Fred had died. Everyone expected Dorothy to sell the house and move in with Tom. Everyone was wrong.

Dorothy recovered quickly. She did not want to move; she would not sell the house. While she tried to be tactful in explaining herself, she had no desire to live with young grandchildren. She liked the quiet environment of her little town where she had lived her entire life. Her sister lived only a few blocks away, and they visited for coffee several times a week. She enjoyed her trips to the post office to retrieve her mail each day. There would be no discussion: she wasn't moving.

Dorothy lived in her home, alone, for 12 years. She suffered a heart attack seven years into that time, and was told by doctors that climbing stairs daily was no longer an option for her. No matter, Tom set up a twin bed for her in the foyer. She slept downstairs for the next five years. Dorothy was safe, she was home, and she was at peace. She did it her way, with no regrets. Tom and his family visited about five times a year, and she visited them for Christmas and Easter. She continued driving her car to the end of her life. Finally, a second heart attack gave final rest to this surprisingly independent woman who had never lived on her own in her whole life, until her husband died.

## Points to Ponder

What's wonderful about this story is that the son heard and respected his mother's choices. They engaged in healthy Family Speak, and he was free to let her live and die as she chose. When she died, Tom and his family were sad, but he had no regrets. He'd grown up in that town himself and understood her attachment to it. Respect for each other suggests that all choices should be considered before life decisions are made.

Tom and his mom lived 200 miles from each other, about a four-hour drive. They visited at least six times a year and talked on the phone twice a week. What would happen if a parent lived a thousand miles away and disliked airplanes? The outcome would be directly related to the quality of the Family Speak. All decisions are unique to each family situation. If the adult children respect their parents' wishes and the parents are open to some compromise, a wide range of options arise. Once the shoulds get in the way, however, the outcome is far more limited.

## A Daughter's Long-Time Hope

Sally, a former client, became estranged from her mother many years ago. She was an only child of parents who divorced when she was a baby. Her dad had disengaged himself physically and emotionally. Sally never saw him and rarely spoke to him. She seldom visited with her mom, either, although she did connect occasionally with her by phone. As Sally tells the story, her mother had money and lived the life of a socialite in a big city, with little need for a young daughter except to criticize her. Sally talked about the many times, when she still lived at home, her mom would find fault with her and tell her friends that Sally was a disappointment to her.

Sally knew in her heart of hearts that one day she would have to move away, which eventually she did. She married a good man and raised three children. Still, she was haunted by the absence of parents in her life. Phone calls with her mom were predictably disquieting, disrupting Sally's peace. As a result, Sally reached out to her mom less and less; her mom rarely initiated the connections.

Recently, Sally's mom, in her late 80s now, had a serious accident. She had been deteriorating emotionally and mentally for some time, but she had hidden her situation from her daughter, using her personal wealth to purchase care. When a serious fall on ice caused her multiple fractures, everything changed. She needed more care than friends could provide. Sally was called, and she readily stepped up to the plate.

Sally brought her mother out of the city to her ranch, creating a lovely apartment for her over the garage. The room was soft and feminine, light and airy, with easy access. Sally was eager to care for her mom, secretly hoping to repair the wounds of the past.

The wounds have not healed. In addition to her mom's physical challenges, local doctors told Sally that her mother suffers from a bi-polar disorder, which requires daily medication. Since she takes her medications irregularly, she is unstable and ill-tempered most of the time. No more dribs and drabs of criticism. Instead, she calls her city friends, reporting that she is a prisoner in her daughter's house. She asks them to come get her and protect her money from Sally. Once, she tried five times in the same week to redo her will with the same attorney.

Some of the people her mother calls keep Sally in the loop. A doctor's visit has recently confirmed early stages of dementia. With this in mind, Sally works hard to love and forgive, to accept her mother as she is. Yet, the little inner child peeks out time and again, craving that elusive affirmation from a mother now caught up in her own isolated world.

Unfinished business abounds. Having waited over 43 years for a smidgen of love from at least one of her parents, Sally relished the opportunity to care for her mom. "Maybe now . . . " she thought. "Maybe now Mom and I can find something special." Imagine her sadness when her mom's naturally self-centered and critical style became all the more tainted by her mental and physical illness. Sally did the right thing, but the outcome was still wrong.

This story continues to unfold. Sally and her mom are dealing with many changes. Sally may not get the love and affirmation she craves, but she has created an interesting scenario. To address her mom's need for physical therapy, Sally has placed her mom in a nursing home about 60 miles from the ranch. There, she receives good care and daily therapy. Despite her mom's inclinations to call old friends in the city and ask for rides home, Sally has made some inroads. She visits two times a week, brings gifts that are appreciated, and occasionally has a real conversation, however brief, with her mom. It's not what Sally has wanted—it's exhausting and consuming, even with nursing home living. Still, the arrangement, which will lead to long-term care in the same facility, is working. Sally is coming to terms with her inner longings and knows in her heart that her mother is not capable of loving her the way she desires. That's okay.

Interestingly, Sally's mom has fared better in the nursing home than she did on the ranch. She seems less disquieted and reactive to Sally in that larger venue. Necessity placed her in the appropriate setting where she could thrive.

Doing the right thing has many faces for our aging parents. Sally understands her mom's limitations now and works with her strengths. Quite possibly, Sally and her mom will be closer to each other during this period of time than they ever have been in 25 years. The unexpected fall brought them together. Time will show what they can do with this potential gift.

## Points to Ponder

Most of us will connect with our parents in their elder years, whether or not we've had a good relationship with them as children or young adults. For some, the candid conversations with our aging elders will be fraught with unspoken opinions on both sides, along with a lack of trust and mutual resentment. They need us, but don't know how to let us in. We need them, but don't know how to heal old wounds. Sally found that, in addition to bringing her mom gifts and taking her on outings, staying on practical topics and activities was a useful beginning. She limited the time she spent with her mom, to guard against engaging in more controversial topics or resurrecting the guilt she had worked so deliberately to keep at bay.

Some of us would be inclined to place a challenging, outspoken, demanding, and unforgiving parent in a nursing home and disconnect emotionally from them. For some of us, that separation may be absolutely right—but not for all of us. If we give power to the hurt feelings that lie beneath such a decision, we may still end up haunted by our unhealed wounds. Sometimes, *doing the right thing* for a difficult parent invites us to let go of the past, even if the parent cannot join us on that healthier plane. If we heal, then we may not have to carry our own unfinished business into old age for our children to deal with.

Positive outcomes become possible when we move beyond the limitations of the past to embrace whatever is possible in the present.

Working with our siblings through the many decisions necessary for our parents' care can bring up a host of old issues; it can also open a new chapter in the family that will draw everyone closer. Either way, family dynamics take the forefront. What might emerge in your own family over parental care decisions?

# 7

## Siblings

### *Shared Genes, Differing Values*

The world changes in part when your parent dies. It changes further when your surviving parent is incapacitated, and it changes forever when both parents are gone. If you have siblings, who you were to each other is predicated on existing authority figures . . . to whatever degree your parents were so. When you must relate to each other without intermediaries, in other words as true equals, it can be like starting from the beginning. Without Mom or Dad to take a side, siblings can't leverage parental support to claim the upper hand in a discussion.

Who do you and your siblings want to be with each other? Without a mom to say, "Did you call your brother for his birthday?" or "Thanksgiving will be at our house this year," you have to decide whether you want to call that brother for his birthday or invite others to make Thanksgiving plans. What meaning does family have for you, apart from doing the right thing because Mom goaded you all to love each other? Honest and deep reflections help you decide what energy you want to devote toward family, and then make the relationships happen.

In my own family, we continue to relate to each other much as we did before, albeit loosely, twice a year or so at someone's home for a long weekend or holiday meal. We do honor birthdays with a phone call, but our worlds were largely joined by our mother and no longer are. We knew about details of our diverse lives because we heard about them through her. Now that the switchboard is not operative, it's definitely more work to stay current with each other's daily lives.

The changes for our family as brothers and sisters began with the car crash. My siblings and I had jobs to do; it was not the right time to figure out our future relationships with each other. Some of us stepped up to the plate more quickly, while others of us felt we were being "ordered around," and so we slowed down even more. Once we learned how to work with one another, no major disagreements defined our time together.

The New Jersey families did most of the regular work: they tended to Dad, dealt with the nursing home staff and then with the assisted living staff; they visited Dad regularly as their own schedules permitted. Jim was in charge of managing Dad's finances. John took the lead for working with attorneys. Jeanne visited almost daily, fed Dad treats, and made friends with the care managers on Dad's behalf. Everyone had a full plate. Occasionally, we felt weighed down by our own load. On any given day, when our own little worlds wore us out, it was easy to think that our siblings weren't doing their share. Some of us had strong opinions about what the others should be doing.

For the most part, though, these mumbles and grumbles dissipated after a good night's sleep and a renewed decision to work with Dad the way that each of us could, without judging what anyone else was or wasn't doing. Our largely separate lives also gave us our own space, making it easier to deal with minor annoyances. This way of thinking became the foundation of our success. We let go and focused on what we alone could contribute.

I am aware that not every family has this experience. On one end of the spectrum are families with tighter bonds—they are each other's best friends. Many other families, on the other end, are quite distant. Their children live separate lives even before their parents die, leading to a very different dynamic when responsibilities are delegated for tasks such as funerals and estate settlements. How they will relate in years to come can't be predicted.

We were lucky that our strengths led us to very different roles in Dad's care. The more roles overlap, the more competition impedes progress, hurt feelings override logic, and tensions block good Family Speak.

The stories below highlight different kinds of family dynamics. For many families, rivalries abound, much is left for others to do (in this case, women), and hurt feelings interfere with the caregiving. One family maintained their connections until their last parent died, then allowed their relationships to degenerate into a mess the very night of the funeral. Their experience points to a challenge that all siblings face. Unfinished business accumulates. When fatigue sets in, it takes very little to overload the system. One wrong word, and hidden grievances lingering below the surface burst forth.

Yet, in the stories below, conflict of this nature was not the norm. Surprisingly, love and loyalty dominated in two out of the three situations. What might you expect to occur when your own family is in crisis?

## When Long-Distance Siblings Are Close and Local Ones Distant

Suzy and Bill's parents lived in New Mexico. While Suzy lived in Ft. Lauderdale, Bill, her brother, lived 90 miles from his parents. Suzy flew to New Mexico every three months for a long weekend, often to find her parents' home in disarray and the cupboards bare. This elderly couple had not aged well. They were both physically frail, weary on life's journey, and not able to tend to each other effectively. Yet, they were not so ill that a nursing home should be considered. They were simply losing their zest for life as the care of their home (as well as themselves) fell to the bottom of their to-do lists. All too frequently, her mom was not bathed, and housekeeping had long since been abandoned. Suzie would call her brother to find out why he hadn't overseen their parents' care during the months since she'd last visited. Bill would change the subject as often as Suzy would allow it. But when he could no longer avoid her questions, he'd try to blame their parents. "They won't let me do anything," he'd retort. In truth, he froze when he visited. He hated seeing them so old and frail, and couldn't wait to leave. Yet, Bill never shared with Suzy any of these private thoughts.

Suzy owned her own business in Florida and was not free to tend to her parents full-time. Her mom and dad wouldn't move away from their land. What could she do? Suzy's only choice was to count on her brother to help their parents and to visit quarterly. She did this for two years. Their mother's health was now failing fast, and their dad, significantly disabled, too, refused to leave their home. During one more trip when her brother had not visited them at all during her absence, Suzy's frustration reached a breaking point, and she and her brother had a blow-out. Frustrated as well, Bill finally told his sister he couldn't stand being in their parents' home, and felt incapable of helping them. As a result, he could only focus on his own life.

The confrontation between these siblings revealed that they had little in common, did not understand each other's ways, and Bill, at least, felt ordered around by his sister. When she left town, he shut her out of his mind, too.

Suzy recognized the problems existing between them, yet she could not break through her brother's defenses; there seemed to be no right answer for the situation. All she knew was that her parents needed care; she was the only go-to person open to them, and she lived a plane ride away. So, although her money was tight, she dug into her own funds to hire caregivers to tend to her parents' personal and medical needs. She expected to be reimbursed with monies from the estate.

Nothing happened as she planned. Suzy's parents died within a few months of each other, in their early 80s. Suzy's brother had enticed their dad to sign papers buying property in the mountains during the few months he lived in the home alone after his wife died. Consequently, there was no estate, no inheritance, no reimbursement. There was only a piece of property in Suzy's brother's name. Exhausted, Suzy didn't put up a fight. She took care of the funeral, the selling of the house, and the purchase of the headstones. She charged these costs to the estate; the funds would come out of her brother's newly purchased land, if he ever sold it. Suzy got on a plane and went home. That was five years ago . . . they were unable to engage each other in a candid conversation that bore any fruit. They haven't spoken since.

## Points to Ponder

Family dynamics today are entrenched in roots from yesterday. Any comment on this brother-and-sister story would require knowledge of the family's past. On the surface, the sister appears to carry the responsibility for her parents, maybe even fulfilling a victim role, and the brother appears to be a selfish son-of-a-gun. And possibly, these appearances are accurate. But who knows what neglect or abuse the brother endured with one or both of his parents that might have made him so reticent to help. What justified (in his eyes) his securing of property for himself before their dad's death? What was it was like for him to be his sister's brother? We only have a glimpse of all this through Suzy's reporting. Who knows what thoughts filled his mind as he faced his parents' dying?

Judging each other's motives is the worst activity for family members to engage in. We may not like someone's chosen behavior or their defense mechanisms, and we may have to make decisions to compensate for them, but we truly do not know another person's heart. I can only reiterate the value of Family Speak. Honest communication may be even more necessary among adult siblings after a parent's death.

In the end, no matter what motives are involved, each caregiver can only do what he or she is capable of doing. In the story above, Suzy has a life to lead, and she has to exercise care not to become a martyr simply because her brother cannot be involved in keeping their mom and dad safe. Without letting go of her values, she could have been more creative and found support early on in the system, through volunteers from various institutions: among them, church, Medicare, home health nursing, and perhaps a once-a-week housekeeper who could perform a range of essential duties. Ultimately, she did engage an array of community and health services. Why she didn't do so sooner remains unanswered.

It's possible that Suzy was silently holding her brother accountable for their parents' unmet needs, and judging him became her own stumbling block. She might have allowed their parents to go without certain services expecting her brother to do the right thing. Surely, she may have thought, he would not let them suffer.

If you have siblings, your job is to take care of yourself, make the best decisions you honestly can, and trust that your brothers and sisters are doing the same. You aren't letting anyone off the hook merely because you have the skill to organize your parents' care. You are recognizing your own abilities, and working around your own limitations. At the end of the day, the only person you can and should control is yourself. The only person you are accountable for and to is yourself. So do what you can: make the calls if you are able, and visit your parents whenever possible. Be who you are, and make peace with the family you were born into.

## Love in the Face of Dysfunction: "Mom Loved You More."

Jill (a former client) has a sister who is three years younger than she is. Their parents divorced before they were in grade school. Their mother, Dotty, adored Jill's sister Donna, who was the baby, but for some reason she couldn't relate well to her older daughter. Jill was sent to boarding school, while Donna stayed home with Dotty. Their dad housed Jill on vacations and holidays for many years, until his own self-centeredness overtook him; he quietly slid into the background of both his daughters' lives before they married.

Despite the obvious favoritism that increased over the years, Donna and Jill formed a good sisterly relationship. Jill knew not to blame Donna for her mother's distortions; Donna knew not to talk too much about Dotty to Jill. The women shared stories of their children, instead, occasionally sharing family vacations, too. Once a year, Donna and her family visited Jill; and once year Jill and her family visited Donna.

Because they raised their children differently, disagreements about discipline or choices emerged from these visits. Donna tended to be laissez-faire and enabling of her children, proclaiming that her offspring were not at all indulged or pampered. Jill saw Donna's choices otherwise. Donna tried to tell Jill to loosen the reins from time to time and allow her children to learn from their mistakes. Jill, tending toward overprotection, did not take well to these suggestions. Still, the sisters did not let these differences intrude on the friendship they had developed with each other.

Jill lived almost 38 years believing that she was not loved by her mother. Even as an adult, married with children, she experienced her mother's animosity. One year, for Christmas, her mom sent her coal in a stocking—no humorous note, no explanation, just a lump of coal. She would regularly forget her grandchildren's birthdays, yet she would call in a drunken stupor when Jill did not send a card from them on her birthday. Jill, ever patient, tolerated her mother's outbursts, and after a few minutes found a way to say goodbye. On rare occasions, her mom would call lucid, kind, and open to Jill's world. Jill took these calls and occasionally made some herself, because she lived for these unexpected joyous moments.

In the course of their back-and-forth, emotionally draining relationship, Jill came to realize that Dotty, once a regular drinker, had become an active alcoholic who was in emotional, physical, and psychological distress. She also knew that feeding the alcohol habit would hasten her mom's death, so she begged Donna, who lived closer to their mother, to cut the funds that were feeding her addiction. Donna couldn't do what Jill asked; she couldn't say "no" to her mother. Instead, she made sure that, every month, their mom had money for . . . whatever.

Donna's constant enabling of their mom became a problem between the sisters during the last few years of their mother's life. Dotty would visit Donna in New York but wouldn't allow either daughter to visit her in Vermont. It was, therefore, impossible for Jill to see the symptoms of progressing alcoholism in her mom's disquieting living conditions. When their mother died, the sisters traveled together to Vermont. Open-mouthed, they surveyed the less than sanitary home in which their mom had lived. They held onto each other and cried. At that point, Donna realized that Jill had been right: out of love, she had been duped into supporting her mom's addiction. Jill, on the other hand, saw unexpected signs that her mom had loved her more than she had ever expressed. All over the cluttered little house, Jill found treasures from her history that her mom had kept safe despite her disintegrating health.

Throughout the visit, the sisters related well to each other—until the funeral, when a seemingly petty detail threatened their connection. Jill found a large poster that Donna and her children had constructed. She'd called it the "Donna and Dotty Show." The poster was filled with pictures of Donna's family and their mom, Dotty . . . that was all. There were no photographs of Jill, her children, aunts, or other family members. The sisters had a row over it. Donna couldn't see Jill's perspective, let alone recognize a problem. Her own grief at the loss of her mom flooded her consciousness. Tempers flared and then subsided. Jill and her family made a new poster, starting with Donna's pictures. They gathered other photographs from aunts and uncles for this second display, and included Jill's family, too. This second poster was the only one displayed at the funeral. Donna never said another word about pictures.

A few days later, the will was read. Jill discovered that she'd been written out of it. She was not totally surprised. Years before, her mother indicated that she might take such a step, when Jill courageously refused to support her drinking habit and distanced from her.

Still, hearing that she had been excluded from the will hurt. Donna was to inherit everything . . . such as it was. Similar parental decisions have ended countless sisterly relationships, and this one could easily have ended theirs as well. It didn't . . . because Jill and Donna didn't let it. This was not about Donna. This was about their sick mom and her limited capacity to deal with reality. Donna, who had been appalled when she read that Jill had been disinherited, worked with Jill and an attorney to rearrange the distribution from the sale of the old house to include her sister. All differences between the sisters crumbled into the dust of their mom's unkempt home the moment they buried their mother. Together, Jill and Donna worked out the details. Donna made sure that Jill received half of all proceeds. As it turned out, mom's home might have been a pigsty, but the land on which it lay was quite valuable. All the grandchildren would have funds for college.

Donna and Jill have resumed their regular phone calls and intermittent visits to each other's homes. They speak kindly of their mom, praying that she might find eternal rest at last.

## Points to Ponder

There are many details to this story. We could psychologize for hours about the effects of divorce, neglect, alcoholism, extended family interventions, and a father's emotional distance. But they all lead us to the same place. These girls had to deal with the death of a mother whose illness had destroyed her life, impaired her relationships with many in the family, and blocked her from loving any of them as they deserved. Even Donna was not loved well. She was the baby and fed off that status. Moreover, every month, with dollars and intentional blindness, she bought her place in her mom's liquid heart.

The quality of the sisters' relationship is what touches us deeply. Despite their differences and varying stances on dealing with addiction, they loved each other, each other's children, and each other's spouses. Their parenting styles were, not surprisingly, at opposite poles, affecting some of their visits, but all in all, they did well with each other.

When their mother's will was read, the sisters' relationship could have ended abruptly. But despite the way these women had been raised, the strength of their love did not let their mother's decisions divide them. Jill accepted her mother's written word; Donna did her best, given her mother's decisions, to treat Jill well.

The sisters and their families continue to visit once a year. They talk on the phone regularly. Life goes on.

## The Family Meeting: When a Parent Takes Charge

Victoria, a former client, retired from a high government position at age 60 to travel and see the world. Three years later, she was stricken with Parkinson's disease. The disease caught her off-guard, but it caught her family even more so.

Victoria is a single parent with a daughter and two sons. Her daughter, who is in her late 20s, lives about 50 miles from her mom. She's a nurturing young woman and often present to her mother, despite her own emerging career. Victoria's oldest son, age 39, is married with two children and lives in Maine. He's the go-to guy in the family. The middle son, in his early 30s, recently moved to Florida. Despite his natural intelligence, he is somewhat lacking in direction and ambition.

Pragmatic, thoughtful, and direct, Victoria saw that her kids were terrified to acknowledge how ill she was. She had already endured several seizures that had sent her to the emergency room. More would surely come. Sometimes, her body froze up. She suffered considerable back pain, lack of muscle strength in her neck that made her head hang or even bob on occasion, and a slowness of gait that sometimes put her off-balance. It became obvious that she would not be able to live on her own much longer. The children needed to face reality. She asked me if I would help her help the children recognize the seriousness of the situation.

I suggested that we convene a family meeting. I would be glad to facilitate, but it would be Victoria's meeting. I encouraged her to think in detail about her goals:

- What did she want to say to her children?
- What did she want to hear from them?
- What kind of outcome did she desire from such a gathering?

Victoria liked the questions. She took them home to ponder, as was her way. The family would be gathering at her home for Christmas. Would I be willing to come to her home and meet with them there over the weekend? I agreed.

When the time came, the family showed remarkable openness. This surprised me because, based on their mom's assessment, I had expected to meet resistance and have to pull and tug information out of them. On the contrary, they were relieved that their mom had called them together, and they welcomed my facilitation. All of them had been harboring private thoughts that required airing before their mom and each other. Her concerns, too, needed to be raised. The meeting lasted 90 minutes.

With the conversation unfolding, several issues came to light. Although she did her best to speak diplomatically, Victoria's daughter was afraid that her brothers would disappear from the scene and that, in essence, she would get stuck as her mom's primary caregiver. The middle brother suggested that he could move back to Virginia, live with his mom in her home, and take care of her there. She probed for specific details of how he'd handle her progressive illness. He could handle her the way she was, he said. He could mow the lawn, buy groceries, and help her to church. Not enough, Victoria rejoined, thanking him for his offer. His responses revealed his limitations in caring for a more debilitated mother. The elder son from Maine thought that no one wanted to talk about his mom's illness. He had decided to be respectful and keep his mouth shut. Once we began the meeting, however, he formulated lots of questions and wanted to know what his role could be.

Victoria and I had talked half a dozen times prior to this meeting. She was well primed for what she wanted from each of her children. She knew their respective strengths and what they could handle. This advanced knowledge, coupled with her natural down-to-business style, served her well. She asked her older son to redesign her home office so that she could maneuver her computer when her fingers stopped flexing. He was skilled with computers and the use of voice recognition technology. She asked the other two to help her find assisted living quarters that would allow her to continue to be independent. She didn't want to live with either of them, but she did want to live near them. Were they in a position to commit to an area of the world for a few years? Yes, they said, and readily agreed to research housing.

Victoria spoke quietly about the deterioration that would ensue. She did not know how long she could live independently. They all asked questions but mostly wanted to assure her that she'd be fine for ten years. Victoria was skeptical of their conclusions, sensing denial at work. So she pressed on. "Listen, children, I may not have ten years. I may not even have five years. But I want these years to be good ones for all of us. I will not burden you. But I will need your help. I want you all to feel free to talk with me as we move along. I don't need to be excluded from discussions. That's why we've had this meeting today. I want it to be the beginning of many. Will you commit to more talking time with each other and with me?" Yes, they readily replied.

This session with Victoria's family confirmed my gnawing desire to chronicle many families' journeys. Talking together was necessary for Victoria and her children. Family Speak began that day for a family that desperately wanted to speak freely with each other but lacked a starting point until the meeting. Yes, they had different apprehensions. How wise and brave of their mother to ask them directly—each one of them—what those fears were. She could no longer bear the silence and denial that surrounded her situation. It was time to throw open the windows and let in some fresh air. Once they started talking, the rest was easy . . . because Victoria *made* it easy. No comment was wrong. No comment was bad. No comment oozed guilt. And yes, the children promised to continue the hard conversations with their mom, as they moved along with this disquieting disease.

## Points to Ponder

Over the years, I have loved client after client . . . all the same. All of them have touched my heartstrings powerfully. Yet every now and then, someone comes along whose story goes to my core. I will never forget them, I celebrate the life in them, I deeply respect their courage in the midst of their personal storms, and I smile broadly when I think of them. Victoria is one of those people.

Victoria was smart, wise, and practical. She accepted her disease and its paralyzing aspects. She was filled with life and soul. I often told her it was time for her to write her story. She could dictate it into the computer, and it would become a bestseller.

With Parkinson's disease, it was right for Victoria to take the lead and bring her frightened adult children into her new reality. Perhaps they thought if they didn't speak about the disease, it wouldn't be real. But it was real, and its deteriorating consequences had to be anticipated.

I was happy to participate in that family gathering. Once we started, the meeting ran itself. The three adult children of this wonderful woman proved to be wonderful themselves. They were honest, open, and direct with their mom about their strengths and limitations. They told her their fears. As time moved on, they followed through on what was suggested at the meeting. Victoria sold the house, and the kids found a great assisted living complex near the daughter's home. The middle son moved close enough to be her driver and companion as needed. The daughter never again felt trapped into being her mom's only caregiver. And the older son became mom's feet and fingers as he masterfully designed unique, technologically advanced stations for her computer workspace and kitchen.

The family was ready to help each other. They just needed a nudge to talk about life, in its many stages . . . together! Bravo to them all!

If you come from a family that also needs to find a starting place for Family Speak, what might be your first step? How could you engage your own family in an open dialogue about upcoming changes and choices? Would it be helpful to bring a professional in, one whom you trust to empathize with you and with the other members of your family, to facilitate a meeting? Can you think of the best setting for such a conversation, one that puts everyone at ease? There may not be the threat of an advancing Parkinson's disease in your family, but the particulars don't matter. What does matter is that silence with sick and aging family members never solves a problem. Someone, anyone, in the family can break the ice and make a difference for everyone down the road.

## The Twins: A Story of Loyalty

Some people mature at early ages. Doing the right thing with their siblings and others comes naturally. Perhaps the following story will strike a chord with you.

Jack (a friend) and his identical twin, Tom, were born into a middle-class Nebraska family 63 years ago. In his prime, Dad had worked as an engineer on the railroad. Their older brother, Vince, died in a train crash at age 18, leaving their sister, Barbara, now 65, as their only older sibling. She lived not far from the family homestead.

Jack's mom died of a stroke in 1992, at age 76, after surviving a difficult bout of breast cancer and another one with colon cancer. She was weary and ready to go. Dad lived until the year 2000, when prostate cancer metastasized into his bones, leaving the three siblings to fully redefine the family.

Tom had not been well for a long time. He'd managed to complete college and spend a couple of years in the Navy before his paranoid schizophrenia was diagnosed. Since then, he has spent his life in the mental health system.

At the time their mother died, the brothers had fallen out of touch. Tom was in a hospital somewhere, but despite Jack's best efforts, he could not locate his twin brother. Tom's previous disappearances had worried Jack considerably, but he eventually found that Tom would come home when he was emotionally able to do so. So, he no longer worried too much about it. Instead, on this occasion, he did the next best thing. Convinced his brother needed to grieve the loss of their mother, he videotaped the funeral. When Tom resurfaced, the brothers watched the video together. And together they cried. Some time later, when their dad lay in hospice growing weaker by the day, Jack flew back to Nebraska from his D.C. home to spend time with him. When Tom called him, as he did on unpredictable occasions, Jack told him that their dad was dying. Tom decided to come home to say goodbye. Jack knew this would be challenging for both father and son. After a few days of his own vigil with his dad, he asked his father if he could bring Tom in to say goodbye. Dad wasn't sure it was the right choice, because Tom usually became agitated around him, but he reluctantly agreed. Tom and his dad spent an afternoon together. It was enough for both of them. It was good; it was loving; and once again, Jack made it happen.

Although Tom was able to stay in town for the next few days, he didn't go to the funeral. He didn't need to. He had his memory.

Barbara and Jack had been named co-executors of their dad's estate. Their dad had taken care of every need. He'd updated the headstone, designed the funeral, and spoken to the kids about his will, his living trust, and his wishes. He was a thoughtful man. As co-executors, Jack and Barbara were in charge of dispensing his desires. But Jack could not do everything his dad had asked. Dad wanted to give Jack a greater inheritance than his brother. Jack told Barbara that this would not be fair or loving. No, he wouldn't do that to his brother. Together, they changed the will to include Tom equally.

Jack has always looked out for his "big" brother (all of 46 minutes his senior). In recent years, he's bought Tom a cell phone to keep him on the map. Tom calls Jack on occasion, but he takes his brother's calls when he is stable and returns them at a later date when he is not. He likes getting phone calls!

After their dad's funeral, fifteen family members, including Tom, gathered for a family photo. Since their father had been a collector of hats, they each wore one of his hats for the picture. Instead of taking their hats off, they put them on and all said at once: "Hats on to Dad!" Jack had a picture framed for Tom as a memory. Tom has no idea where the picture is right now, but he remembers receiving it. That's what matters.

### Points to Ponder

I have met numerous families with mentally challenged members. Many of them feel burdened by the one who is not well. They do right by their loved one, but the effects of the disease wear them down. A child, brother, or sister squanders the funds they've been given; they disappear for years or start a fire in the apartment someone has furnished for them; they call from jail. Some people because of their internal struggles can look like "takers." Their abilities to adequately give and receive love are often compromised. They are limited in their capacities to interact and lack the freedom to show the love they have inside.

Jack has not been deterred by any of Tom's ways. He loves his brother deeply, compensates for his shortcomings, and includes him in his plans . . . whether or not Tom shows up. Tom will return from time to time—he always does. There is no evil in him. He is simply unable to stay medicated long enough to stay well. Brother to brother, the bond is rock-solid. This kind of love and patience is a gift of Grace.

Jack's deep empathy with his brother is related to being a twin; perhaps, Jack thinks that if life had zigged instead of zagged, he'd be the one with the struggles that now weigh Tom down. Perhaps, he believes that he owes his brother his lifelong loyalty and love. I don't know the answer. What I do know is that it takes great love to sustain such a commitment. Such love is always associated with a higher spiritual plane. Whoever finds that plane is blessed and can bless those they love.

Death will have her say with us all. Whether or not our families prepare together for the final days, we will all have to decide what we will do, whether or not we will be present, and what our siblings mean to us after our parents are gone. What are the different ways parents approach death? How do we, as their children, let them do so?

# 8

## Saying Goodbye Openly
### *Sharing the Sacred Journey*

Every parent has a different way of saying goodbye to their family. In my own family, one parent, my mother, was easy to understand. My father challenged us to look for the clues. Because my parents represent the opposite ends of the spectrum, I want to share their stories at length, then offer other stories that show diverse ways parents have of being in the world and preparing to say the ultimate goodbye.

### Marie's Story

Mom was a spiritually strong, traditional Catholic woman, and she liked to talk about her faith with others. While sick, she turned to the TV for spiritual comfort through masses, rosaries, and other religious programs. She read *Catholic Digest* and spoke often about the Blessed Mother, God, and death. This kind of talk was not easy for my siblings, probably because they were not as engaged in their religion; they sometimes wearied of the constant references to church. Also, mom's words were usually followed by some comment about her eventual death, and no one else wanted to engage mom in conversations about that. Talking about faith and God's love was a common aspect of my life and work, however, and so I found it easier to share in that way. I listened attentively for the ways God was preparing her for the afterlife. Sometimes, in fact, we'd talk for hours about the presence of God.

Mom wasn't afraid of death. She believed in an all-loving God who would welcome her. She expected death and anticipated God's embrace. She was, however, terribly afraid of the dying *process*. She didn't want to waste away with cancer, a process she had seen others endure. Yet, she understood that this might become her fate. Nervously, she mentioned these dreads to me, but more often she spoke positively of a life well-lived, her gratitude to God for granting her the family she cherished, the children she always wanted, and a husband who had loved her for over 61 years. None of her children had died early; life was good. She was ready to go whenever God called her.

Mom and I spoke of her cancer. She showed me her distorted breast and the progression of the disease. I had researched inflammatory breast cancer to prepare myself to view what I didn't wish to see. Mom's breast was indeed as ugly as the pictures I'd seen. But I kept a straight face and asked gentle questions—"Hmmm . . . is it sore? Is the chemo helping? Can you sleep on your left side?" and questions of that nature. Mom watched me carefully for adverse reactions. The last thing she needed was for me to feed her already growing fear by showing distress. I watched the cancer spread from ugly to leprous. Then, I watched as the sores seemed to dry up and appear less raw. Through it all, I watched the chemo ravage her body but never her soul.

At various times, when the chemo lowered her blood count so severely that we feared she wouldn't survive the night, mom and I talked about her funeral. It was one thing to discuss death and God in the abstract—it was quite another to talk explicitly about my mother's funeral with my mother! She told me what outfit she wanted to wear and who it was most important for me to call because they were off dad's list and unlikely to be notified otherwise. I took good mental notes. Mom told me she wanted a closed casket and didn't want folks gawking at her shell of a body. She wanted to be cremated after the funeral.

Mom loved each one of us in a special way. I visited monthly for two years, while many different treatments were tried. At the end of each visit, I was not sure I'd ever see her again. Repeatedly, mom told me she loved me, and she singled out what she valued about me, what she thought was special about me. I know that during her last two years, she told every one of us some variation of these words. It was awkward for me to hear her pour forth her love. I cherished hearing her thoughts about my life and my choices. Yet at the same time, I was embarrassed. I wanted to hear more, as much as she wanted to say, and at the same time I wanted her to stop!

Today, I am infinitely appreciative that she spoke to me as she did. I will hold her comments in my heart forever. I have no regrets with mom . . . mostly because she made sure we had our talks. Whether they were embarrassing or not, mom didn't stop until she'd said all she wanted me to remember. I hope that I will be able to do the same with my own family when my time comes.

After mom's death, despite dad's fragile state in intensive care, the horror of the accident dictated that *we* needed a funeral. Our families, their friends, even local townsfolk—everyone needed a funeral.

I was selected to plan the service with the church ministry team. I knew the songs Mom wanted sung; the Scripture she wanted read; and the flowers she would prefer. I was happy to plan the Mass of the Resurrection, and still, it was extremely painful. Brother John accompanied me to the florist, the church, and the funeral home. Even prepared, we were not prepared. I *knew* her wishes, yet I could barely concentrate on the tasks at hand. After a loss of that proportion, my mind couldn't hold it all.

My four brothers alternated care of Dad, making sure that someone was at his side every minute of every day in the hospital. We were all stretched to the limit emotionally. My sister was the most vocal in her grief. Her wails echoed the ones in all our hearts. Our loss was sudden, horrific, and in no way absorbable.

## Points to Ponder

Several significant messages are embedded in this story.

1. The first regards my mother's *openness to her own journey*. She paced herself along the path by verbalizing the process. If I had not talked with her, she would have found someone else. Perhaps it was nervous anxiety abetted in words; perhaps it was her style of dealing with reality; and perhaps God was preparing her spirit even then. As you meet others like her, I hope you can walk with them at their pace, for a little while, listening and sharing as seems most natural.

2. The second message focuses more directly on mom's spiritual grounding. How marvelous to be so confident in the Love that brought us into being and calls us home. What a blessing to know peace at the end of life's journey. But mom had more than peace. She had joy and gratitude for the life she'd lived, the family she'd loved, and the many other gifts that had

come her way. Watching people who believe so strongly in the presence of God prepare for death is compelling. It is one of those experiences that linger in one's memory.

3. The third message regards the comments mom made to us individually. Those of you who have received those sacred words of affirmation—"I love you", "I appreciate you"—know that they are treasures that surpass all others in life. Some of you may have waited by a bedside for some of those words and never received them. Do not despair. Not all of us are capable of sharing our love in words. I encourage you to look in a different direction. Look to deeds or gifts or pictures. Love has a way of showing itself even when words don't come easy.

4. The fourth message regards planning Mom's funeral with her. At the time, our conversations felt surreal. Today, I appreciate their naturalness. The rituals in the Mass were important to her, and she wanted to envision and embrace the holiness of it all. Since that conversation with my mom, I've listened differently as others have shared with me their family's attempts at such exchanges. Some folks write down their desires because they don't find it easy to talk about them. Others do so because their families are not church goers and wouldn't know how to plan for a church funeral. One woman I knew went to her pastor and told him what she wanted. How it's done is not the important part. The key issue is that you allow your loved ones to share their chosen rituals with you, because embracing this ritual experience is what helps prepare their soul for what's next.

Ultimately, Mom didn't die the way she expected to die, but she knew that her time was coming. As it turned out, death stormed in unexpectedly, and the shock became as much a part of the experience as her death itself for the family.

We all respond differently to these times. Expect it, in yourself and in others. Disbelief and grief mix with the need to make quick decisions, perhaps long-distance travel plans, and confusion about what needs to be done, by whom, and in what sequence. Someone usually steps forward to make some decisions, but these decisions may not take into consideration the needs of others. They can bypass those in the family who need more time to contemplate options before entering into a plan. Shock still lies just below the surface impacting every communication and task.

Below are two brief stories that cause us to think about our own immediate reactions to the unanticipated death of a loved one.

## A Tale of Two Families

Among his three siblings, Charlie lived the closest to his dad when he died. He took it upon himself to set some wheels in motion. By the time his two siblings arrived, he'd arranged transportation from the airport, decided who would stay with whom, set the date of the funeral, written the obituary, and called the newspaper. His siblings accepted his choices. They were thrilled that Charlie was so resourceful.

He was not finished. Charlie decided which of the siblings would deliver a eulogy, who would lead prayer, and who would pick out the coffin and work with the funeral home directors. The only one who balked was the sister chosen to offer the eulogy. She was overwhelmed and thought she'd cry so hard she would not be able to complete her thoughts. No problem. Charlie said he would step in if that proved to be the case.

The family was in a daze through most of the next week. Friends and extended family brought food, helped spread the news, and were available as needed for other tasks. When the funeral was over, Charlie broke down. His siblings had returned to their homes and he was alone. He felt his pain then, and within a short time, he buckled at the knees. There was much to do, but he hadn't asked for help with any of it. He felt responsible for the remaining tasks, such as the sale of the house and other estate details. Why? Well, he was the oldest. Wasn't it his job?

Charlie had done it all. Initially, he was pleased; his family was pleased. All too soon, however, Charlie was a mess. A month after his father's funeral, his wife, noticing his struggle, nudged him to seek grief therapy. That's how I met him.

When Nan's mother died, she and her mother were living in the same town. They had talked a lot about her mom's desires. So Nan felt responsible for carrying out her mother's wishes. When the family gathered, she read them a list of tasks similar to Charlie's list. But in her case, the family mutinied. "You can't tell us what to do. We'll decide together. Who are you to think for any of us?" Nan crumbled into tears; she felt totally misunderstood and dejected. In response, she abdicated all leadership and did nothing for the next week except to show up when expected. Her siblings tried to tell her that her intentions had been good, but that she really didn't have the right to make so many big decisions without consulting them. As a group, but without Nan's input, they assigned the tasks. The family was trying to grieve the loss of their mom, but the rift that had occurred during the week of the funeral divided their energies and distorted all that happened. One of Nan's sisters became my client. She felt she had not had the opportunity to grieve her loss. She had been too uptight about Nan.

## Points to Ponder

We've all met Charlie before. He's a good guy who is super-responsible, eminently able, and perpetually incapable of asking for help. He doesn't know his limits until he reaches them . . . and then he crashes. But this happens so infrequently that he forgets from year to year that it's happened before. Charlie had never experienced the trauma that accompanies a parent's death, so he didn't know how to read the lower speed-limit signs. He plunged ahead until he could go no further. Six months of therapy and anti-depressant medication helped him rethink many of his former choices. He had not only overworked himself—he had overlooked the contributions his siblings could make and the role he could have played in urging them to put their skills to good use.

Nan also meant well. She tried to do what Charlie did. But unlike Charlie's family, her family, less compliant and more proactive, needed to be included in the decision-making, so they couldn't let her dictate their roles. The fact that Nan moved so quickly from one extreme to another, from total control to total abdication of responsibility, tells us about her great need to be valued by her family. She was not free to say, "Sorry guys, I overstepped. Let's regroup and divvy up the tasks together." At a time when the family could least find the energy to stroke her wounded feathers, she became self-centered, and as a byproduct, obstructive to the family process.

The different ways people respond and react to loss is worth pondering. We can't predict for certain what we might do in the future, but we can consider what we have done in the past and, looking back, perhaps come to appreciate the different expressions of grief operative in our own families. With new eyes, we might be able to unearth the good intentions that may have been buried under some poor choices. Nan's family tried to honor her attempts, but her embarrassment over their rejection of her choices blocked her ability to receive their kind words. They did not want to negate their sister—they wanted input. How can we all learn from this for our own future reference? Perhaps, we might make a mental note to pay better attention to our own instinctive reactions, and tune in to those of others before we respond the next time. In this way, we might in greater self-awareness be less likely to exclude, offend, or undermine others who are just like us . . . but different. The greatest goal is to become more compassionate and sympathetic toward others (and ourselves as well) when we don't choose well.

## Misguided Loyalty: We Can Never Protect Ourselves from Death

Annie was one of four adult children who lost their mom at age 69 to a swift and painful disease. No one was prepared. Their mom had been healthy and living independently for several years after her divorce from the children's father. All of a sudden, within a two-week period, she contracted pneumonia that defied treatment and was rushed to the hospital with dehydration. Most of Annie's siblings were in denial and kept waiting for mom to "snap out of it."

No one even considered that mom's life might be in danger. Annie was local, held the power of attorney status, and was the one who got the call from the doctor that her mom had passed away. She was the one who informed the rest of the family. Even though she was not the oldest, Annie believed that it was her job to hold herself together for the others. So she organized the activities and rituals for the family for several days. The funeral was set for five days after her mom's death to give extended family time to travel from out of state. Other siblings did as much as Annie, but they handled different tasks. As a matter of fact, they all did amazing things in a short period of time, with grace and grief mixed together. It would be difficult to single out any one of them as a slacker. Their family loyalty and love kept them together . . . even while they took on separate tasks.

They grieved privately, however. Each went to their respective homes and crashed every night, without sharing their exhaustion with anyone else. Annie crashed the hardest the night before the viewing. She was tired, the tasks were finished for the evening, and her tears were unstoppable. She cried so hard that Carl, her husband, thought she would be sick. Then he did what a lot of husbands might do. He decided to protect his wife. He saw what tasks were on her plate. He saw how overwhelmed *she* was. He felt love in his bones for her and called one of her siblings. He was sure too much was being asked of Annie. He wanted to let the others know that Annie needed a reprieve.

Carl talked with several of the siblings over the next few hours, asking them if they could pick up some more tasks, explaining that Annie was really wiped. What he heard surprised him—mostly, because he had not been attuned to what the others were doing. He found out that they *all* were tired and doing all they could do. The ones he talked with could not find any energy to take on more than their current load. If Annie was at the end of her rope, so were the rest of them.

This was a benign exchange. Carl, like his wife, was not tuned in to what others in the family were accomplishing, but his intentions were meant to be helpful. As a result, he grew in respect for his wife's sisters and brothers, particularly when he realized how they all contributed to the stability of the family unit during that week. The family continued their heroics with each other in an affable manner until all was completed, with Carl himself picking up some tasks that might have been deflected to a sibling if he hadn't asked his questions.

## Points to Ponder

Conversations such as the ones Carl initiated could fall on deaf ears, or worse, generate angry responses. They could divide and polarize a family at a time when togetherness should be at the fore. When anguish consumes us and emotions are raw, logic goes out the window. Even one question at the wrong time could usher in an emotional downslide, destroying potentially well-intentioned exchanges. Such exchanges happen when emotions are high and shock is recent. Many families have a tough enough time communicating their feelings in the easiest of situations. How much more challenging it is with extraordinary events or crises.

Carl's communication style with his brothers- and sisters-in-law saved him from shooting himself in the foot. Once he "got" the broader picture, he could be more helpful to them all. For a few days, it may be impossible to bring our own grief (or that of our spouse) into perspective, but giving others the benefit of the doubt may be vital to sustaining family relationships.

My hope in sharing these stories is to call upon your compassion for your own family members during times of crisis. Quite likely, all of us "lose it" to some extent, taking charge prematurely, becoming overprotective, or getting angry inappropriately during these sacred times. Some families break apart for decades over minor incidents. Empathy, consideration, compassion, forgiveness, short memories, and an attitude of "there but for the grace of God go I" would serve us well.

The stories above focused on the funeral preparation time. From my own perspective, I've found it easier to write about the "after death" time than about my dad's final days on earth. Which set of circumstances would be easier for you to experience?

# 9

## Saying Goodbye Privately
### *Silence on the Sacred Journey*

People have countless styles of communicating, in life and at the end of life. Some write stories, paint pictures, or fill a wall with family photos in their home. Some hint at a serious topic and hope you pick up on it; others are so direct that their words can sting sometimes. The communication continuum is long because, higher level species that we are, communicating well remains a lifelong challenge. My own parents were polar opposites. As open as my own mom was, my dad was closed. As spiritually verbal as Mom was, Dad was silent. As free to express her desires as Mom was, Dad was reserved. This was his way.

### Fred's Story

One day when I was younger, Dad and I went to lunch. Carrying all my new family therapy tools, I invited him to express himself on many subjects, including religion. Having grown up in the wake of the changes in the Catholic Church in the '60s, I wanted to hear where Dad stood on those issues. He told me in one short paragraph: religion is private. He was working out his relationship with God in his own way, and he expected me to do the same. He would not be sharing his relationship with God with me. And he never did . . . not once during the next thirty years.

Dad was not a talker—he was a doer. He took pictures and kept a special album where all our memories are preserved. Dad would shuck clams and corn for hours in preparation for a family feast. He worked tirelessly to lay tile, wallpaper a room, or build a bookcase. His work was always impeccable. Those were Dad's ways. He did not use words but he was present to us if we read between the lines. There we would find dad's intimate expressions. I recalled those memories during Dad's nursing home and assisted living time.

At the assisted living center, the blood infection that Dad had developed when in intensive care continued to defy treatment. One day, my brother Jim called with the painful news that Dad had been diagnosed with advanced leukemia. He had six weeks to live.

Six weeks! Dad had survived the worst of a horrific accident and the loss of my mother and was finally settled. He was primed to enjoy a few years in his new environment. We could not wrap our minds around the diagnosis. It seemed so unfair to him.

When dad was told the news, he heard what he wanted to hear: he had something *like* leukemia, not the real thing. From that day forward, dad talked about having some disease like leukemia, insisting that his life was not in imminent danger.

Dad would not, for one second, discuss his dying with any one of us. Not even I, with my well-honed therapy skills, could get him to mention impending death. I was corrected by him each time I mentioned the diagnosis. My observations and inquiries led me to believe that he shielded himself with denial. Perhaps he could not hold the truth, so he twisted it to become something he could absorb.

I wanted to call Hospice immediately, but my siblings asked me not to introduce Hospice yet. "Why not?" I asked. "Because that will bring to light how ill dad is, and he doesn't want us to be with him on that level," one of them perceptively responded. "We'll honor him better by living in the moment." At first reluctantly, I honored the family's request.

Dad did something interesting after his diagnosis. He wrote letters to eight or ten special people in his life, mostly thank-you notes for their calls and concern for him during the time of his recovery after mom's death. For six months he had talked about writing the letters but had not done so. During this last full month of life he finished the letters. He showed copies of them to any of us who would read them. I'm sure that those who received his letters had no idea dad was saying goodbye in his own fashion. He, of course, knew on some level that his time was limited.

As events played out, all of what happened during those final weeks honored Dad—not my way, but his way. My siblings were right. My way worked for Mom, but not for Dad. Maybe you already know how to honor the differences in your own parents, but I had to learn the hard way. Dad chose his own path.

## Points to Ponder

Mom's story and Dad's story can be illustrative of your own story. Is there someone in your world who will talk openly with the parent who needs to talk, who needs to share their story, who needs to display the ugliness of the disease that ravages them or the fears about dying that confront them? Is there someone in your family who will honor the ways of the parent who is very private? How will you love these people who live life so very differently, who love so very differently, and who choose to die so very differently?

Families have various reactions to Hospice. Some will respond as my family did and hold back the call until the last minute. No decision is right for every situation—the right decision must emerge from family conversations, consultations with doctors, and an assessment of how sick the parent is.

Below are stories that depict different ways of saying goodbye to a parent.

### "Mommy, May I Climb in Bed with You?"

When this story begins, Eileen, a former client, was 48, and her mom was 76. They had become very close, especially after Eileen's dad died. They chatted every day and visited twice a week for coffee or shopping. One day, her mom had a massive stroke. At that moment, she lost her power to speak and her ability to touch her daughter with her hands. Yet, her eyes remained as alert as ever. Through them, Eileen saw life inside her mom's stricken body. Later that same day, the doctors told her that her mother might not survive the devastating event.

Eileen returned to the hospital room and looked into her mother's eyes. Mom knew. Eileen could tell. Mom's eyes were filled with love. "Mommy, can I climb in bed with you?" Eileen asked. With a flutter of the eyelid, her mother said yes. Eileen climbed into the bed with her mother, cuddling her and stroking her face, her arms, and her hair. She sang into her ear softly, while tears streamed down her mother's face. When she finished the song, Eileen again touched her mother's cheek and felt the remnants of a tear.

A nurse came in the room for a routine procedure but quickly changed her mind. She found Eileen sleeping with her arms around her mom. The nurse quietly left the room and didn't return for an hour.

Her mom died early the next morning. Eileen had sung her goodbye. She and her mother shared love to the end.

## Points to Ponder

When we have the opportunity to say goodbye, it is important for us to do so in ways that are true to ourselves and our parents. Eileen hopped into bed with her mom. Others might say things they've never managed to say before, or make sure the dying person knows they are loved. Eileen and Mom already knew that about each other. Eileen needed to hold on, give comfort, and bring grace to the final moments of life.

Some of us live hundreds of miles from our loved ones. How do we love them from afar? How do we connect with them in ways that are meaningful? We need to listen to our hearts and do what will allow us to have peace at the end. Some of us will need to drop our daily activities and rush to our parent's side; others will become creative with Skype, emails, and pictures or notes sent through snail mail. It matters less *what* we do and more *what our choices mean* to us and our parent.

Here are a few examples. For two years, when my own mother was very sick, I was in a position to travel monthly to be with her for a long weekend at a time. When she died, I ached over her irreplaceable loss, but I was at peace. I have friends who email their parents daily; some call weekly and because of the distance, visit less often—once or twice a year. A friend recently suggested that it was time to double his trips to his parents' home a thousand miles away. He knows what he needs to do to be at peace when they pass.

There are no "right" answers, no single solution that can work for everyone, and no map to follow. We have only our own answers that speak to our hearts and the relationships we've had. If they are born out of love, respect, and a sensitive awareness of who we are as individuals and as a family, they are likely to be the right ones.

## "Will You Pray over Me?"

Margaret (a close friend) and Jim divorced after 28 years, for many reasons that she chose not to discuss. Jim had emphysema and smoked heavily to the end of his life. He knew he would die young, but he had chosen his course. He was 61.

Jim's family ostracized Margaret for leaving him. She publicly stood her ground but privately questioned her decision. Did she do the right thing? Did she have the right to leave a sick man?

When Jim was in hospice three years after they divorced, he asked Margaret to visit him. She decided to bring a friend along for support and for prayer. She wasn't sure how Jim's family would receive her. Margaret's prayer community literally laid hands on the sick. Perhaps that would happen this day if Jim so wished.

When Margaret arrived, Jim's family milled around his room and the adjacent waiting room. Jim told them she was coming. So, they welcomed her into their midst. She had not seen most of them during the prior three years.

Jim greeted Margaret and her friend warmly. He opened his arms to his ex-wife, and they held onto each other. Some of the family sat in the corner and quietly observed their intimate moment. Jim told Margaret he was scared; she told him she understood. She told him that God loved him and that she also loved him; he told her that he loved her and that he was sorry he hadn't been a good husband. They both cried. He asked her if she would pray for him.

Margaret produced some holy oil and without a word handed the jar to her friend. By this time, the room was filled with about ten people . . . all from Jim's family. The friend looked around the room with trepidation in her eyes. She had only come to lend her support, not for front line work. Nevertheless, she took the vial and sat on the bed. "God help me," she prayed silently.

Everyone watched as the friend anointed Jim's head, his lips, his hands, and his feet. She asked God to heal all that was not yet whole in his life. She anointed his heart and bid him a safe journey into God. She was not aware that the family was humming "Amazing Grace" in the background.

## Points to Ponder

The difficulty of this deathbed scene was compounded by the unfinished business between Jim and Margaret. Jim gathered the courage to send for his ex-wife. She forgave herself for leaving him. He apologized for not being the husband she deserved. She forgave him his limitations and unwise choices. Jim longed for that peace that surpasses understanding, often the fruit of prayer. He died peacefully in his sleep later that evening.

Many families would benefit from such forgiveness and healing before a loved one dies. This doesn't mean it always happens. It takes enormous grace to set aside pride and old wounds. Because Jim and Margaret both surrendered their armor, they found peace.

## Daddy, Can You Hear Me? I'm Right Outside.

Missy and Diane were sisters whose dad (a long-time friend) was in the final stages of bone cancer. He had been sick for three years. Diane was the older of the two, and she and her mother were at his side regularly. She wanted to drink in his love to the last minute.

Missy was present for the family, too, but in her own way. She helped with the groceries and laundry, and while Mom was at the hospital, took phone messages, and brought in the mail at the family home. During their trips to the hospital, Missy cooked special foods and had them waiting for her parents at dinnertime. Whenever she phoned from home, Missy made Dad laugh during their conversations.

Despite how present she had been, however, when Dad's illness took its final turn, Missy distanced herself. She couldn't bear to watch him die. The last month of his life she visited very little. She called him on the phone and talked with him for a few minutes each time. It was all that she could handle.

The time came when mom called the girls and reported that their dad would probably not last the night. Would they come right away? Yes, they both said. Missy and Diane drove together to the hospice house. Diane went into the room and stayed with her dad and mom. Missy entered dad's room— and froze. She struggled to the bed to give him a kiss, where she paled and felt nauseous. Within a few minutes, Missy stumbled out of the room. Her mother followed and took her to the rest room, put cold cloths on her head, and made her sit down. Mom told her it was okay to be just the way she was. Missy was just as present to Dad outside the room as she might be inside the room. "Dad knows; he understands," her mother said. "Are you sure?" Missy wanted to know. "Yes, my darling. I'm sure," her mom replied. Missy sat outside the room, perhaps 50 feet from her dad's bed. She hoped he could hear her loving thoughts. When Dad died, Missy cried for hours.

## Points to Ponder

I could only wish freedom from guilt for Missy. Her dad knew how much she loved him. She was a devoted daughter in her own distinctive ways. He could not have asked more of her.

How wonderful that her mom, even in the midst of her own grief, could support Missy in her private dilemma. She knew that Missy had a visceral reaction to her dad's dying. Some grief counseling down the road might be useful for Missy to figure out the root cause of her intense anxiety. But for now, all those involved understood Missy's good intentions and allowed her to make peace with her choices.

How would you judge your own reactions to others' limitations with a dying parent? Do you find yourself contemplating how ignorant, incompetent, or self-centered someone is because they can't say goodbye at the bedside? Or do you respond in a similar manner to Missy's mom, who wouldn't think of throwing a guilty dart at her daughter whether or not that daughter could be physically close to her father at the end?

No matter how many scenarios I describe here, many more possible scenarios exist. In sharing these, I have only one intention in mind: to convey my belief that there is no single method for saying goodbye to a loved one. The styles are as numerous as there are people in this world. We need only listen to our own hearts to discern what's right for us.

The events on the weekend of my father's death express, as few other stories that I know of can, the way we might share even the most private person's end-of-life journey. Into this incomparable period are drawn various inner events: the awareness of our own mortality, our beliefs about an afterlife, and the unmistakable sense of a spiritual presence in the hour of death. This time frame is unique unto itself. It is to be experienced by those who are blessed to be with a loved one at the end. Words cannot adequately capture the range of emotions.

# 10

# Now and at the Hour of Death
## Stories from the Final Days of Life

The moment of death is sacred because each human being is sacred. In my dad's story and those that follow, the signs are obvious . . . if you know what to look for.

My dad had been given six weeks to live. During those weeks, he ate little, slept a lot, seemed to remember less, and wearied easily, but none of these were new symptoms. They were merely accentuated. We had expected more changes. "Could the specialist have been wrong?" I asked my siblings.

When I visited on what became the last weekend, no one thought Dad was going to die before another week began. Dad greeted me with a look of surprise, having forgotten that I was coming. Shortly after I arrived, my sister Jeanne stopped by to welcome me. When the manager of the care staff saw us in the entrance hall, he beckoned us into a private room—always a bad sign. He told us that Dad was very ill and that we should call Hospice. When I did so, the after-hours recording gave me an emergency number to call. Not sensing an emergency, I didn't leave a message. But I knew at this point that the staff wanted Hospice in on the care plan. Something was changing. I returned to Dad's apartment with my secret.

Dad and I prepared for dinner. I was determined that we would sit in the dining room that evening. Dad agreed. He wheeled himself into the bathroom and spent over half an hour combing his hair, wanting to look his best. We sat at a table for two in the front section of the dining room. His tomato juice was on the table within minutes. I ordered wine for myself.

During the next hour, I witnessed a most extraordinary occurrence. We inadvertently had chosen a table in the center of the residents' path into and out of the dining room. As folks left, they passed right by Dad, who was facing them. Over a dozen of his fellow residents stopped at the table. They'd missed their friend who had not been among them that week. When they saw us, their faces lit up. This was their chance to say hello. Dad smiled and greeted each one of them, shaking their hands warmly. He was weak and had trouble speaking. He didn't eat at all, but the value of that meal was not in the food they served us; it was in Dad's saying goodbye to his friends, even though neither he nor I knew then that this would be the purpose of the impromptu receiving line.

After dinner, a care manager helped Dad get ready for bed. Around 8 p.m., I said goodnight. Because dad had coughed a lot during the day, I offered to bring lozenges on Saturday morning when I returned.

The floor nurse found me first thing in the morning. "Did you call?" she asked. When I shared with her the recording options, she told me emphatically that this was indeed an emergency. I called again and left a message that was returned an hour later. A Hospice nurse would come to the Center around noon on Sunday.

Dad was more gravely ill than we siblings could detect. The nurse's urgency told me his time was near. In prayer shortly after Dad's diagnosis, I had asked God to let me be with him for his last few days of life. Here it was. I had never walked with anyone through their final stages, so I wasn't sure what I would see, hear, or smell, or what I would do. I only knew that my heart was full, and I wanted Dad to be comfortable.

Dad coughed all day. He couldn't clear his throat no matter how much he tried. He took many naps, for which I was grateful. At least, sleep bought his body a reprieve.

When I spoke to the floor nurse, she explained that his body was breaking down, heart failure was setting in, and the end we expected was near.

Dad didn't eat that day; he didn't dress; he didn't comb his hair or brush his teeth. He had very little energy. He looked at me with a look I couldn't read. He sat in his chair as long as he could to honor my presence and even made jokes from time to time. Then sleep overtook him.

Jeanne and the kids came by during the day. Dad rallied, but his mid-sentence naps made us laugh, bringing a little lightness to our gathering. When Dad awoke, he labored to clear his throat. It never occurred to me that stronger medications would help him rest more comfortably. Even then, I was ignorant of what was happening. I didn't really grasp that his last breath would occur within 36 hours. Our brother John came by for his weekly Saturday sports-on-TV afternoon visit. Dad slept through most of it. John and I talked. John vividly remembers the last words Dad spoke to him. Later, I realized that those who needed to see Dad that weekend saw him.

Nurse Gina from Hospice arrived shortly after noon on Sunday. She took charge from her first gentle but firm hello. "What problems do you have, Fred?" she asked. Dad replied: "Just my foot. I have an infection in my foot that hasn't healed in a year." Nurse Gina looked at me. I shrugged my shoulders. To the end, Dad did not acknowledge his leukemia. Gina began paperwork with Dad and suggested I get some tea. Perhaps I could use a break? For the better part of the next three hours, Gina worked with Dad and the staff nurse. She was kind, yet sharp. The transfer of authority from private physicians to Hospice began. Doctors were called; forms were faxed; and new, stronger drugs were ordered. All this occurred on Sunday evening. Gina stayed at the Center until around 8 p.m. She may have known she'd be back. I still didn't know my day was far from over.

Sometime during the late afternoon, my sister's husband, also called John, came to visit. He loved Dad very much and often came to spend quiet time with him when no one else was around. I was glad for his gentle presence. So was Dad.

Looking back, I am in awe of the serendipitous nature of the events that took place. These events, in their individual ways, seemed to provide a circle of love around Dad as his body prepared for the final shut down.

First, after the consultation with the manager on Friday, Jeanne insisted I stay in New Jersey. "You can't go home, Mare," she said. She felt the urgency more than knew it. I had been scheduled to leave mid-Sunday afternoon and begin seeing clients on Monday at home. Saturday evening she repeated herself in a forceful manner. "You're not going home. That's all there is to it!" I knew she was right, canceled clients, and extended my stay. As it turned out, I did not return home for almost three weeks.

Second, during Dad's interview with Gina, I went down to a bistro for my tea. It was there that I encountered Irish Mary. Mary was a care manager on Dad's floor who knew Dad since his arrival. We all knew Mary. She was loving and kind . . . and very Irish, like our mom. Mary had just returned from a retreat in France at Lourdes and was devastated to hear about Dad's deterioration.

Thinking out loud for ways she could help, she offered to spend the night in Dad's room if we needed her. Later that afternoon, Gina made it clear that Dad should not be left alone. Indeed, we should consider having someone stay with Dad for several nights. Mary had volunteered *even before* I knew she was needed. I accepted her offer.

Third, around 3 p.m., my cell phone rang. The call from this particular old friend was out of the blue; we had not spoken in a year. "Mary Ann, I'm calling because you've been on my mind all weekend. I think your father is very ill. He is very ill, is he not?" When I replied in the affirmative and noted that Hospice was with him at the moment, she continued. "I want you to read the 23rd psalm to him. Don't think—just do it. It is very important. Say it, read it, whatever. Just be sure to say the 23rd psalm to your father today. Will you promise me you'll do this?" I promised—rashly, maybe, but I promised. I trusted the spiritual centeredness of my friend of many years. I poked my head into a few apartments and asked for a Bible. I couldn't find one in the building! None of the dozen folk I asked could produce the sacred Scripture. Later, Irish Mary and I reconstructed the 23rd psalm as best we could, knowing that we were omitting some pertinent lines. What we wrote would suffice.

Fourth, I had made plans for Dad to receive the sacrament of the sick (a Catholic blessing) in preparation for death. One of the managers offered to bring the local priest, who visited the Residence on Sunday mornings, to Dad's apartment. As it turned out, the priest was ill and never arrived. When I told Mary, she put her hand into her jacket pocket and produced a little bottle of holy water from Lourdes. "Would you mind if I blessed your dad with this holy water?" she asked me. My mouth dropped open, tears poured forth, and my head nodded a "yes, thank you!" all in one motion. I thought: "Oh Mom, through the grace of God, you sent Irish Mary to be God's instrument on this priestless Sunday!"

Fifth: And so it happened. It was 5 p.m. on a Sunday in 2006. Dad was exhausted. Gina was busy ordering new medications. Mary helped dad into his pajamas, and then she and I helped him into bed. She extracted the holy water from her pocket and asked Dad if she and I could pray with him. He nodded his head yes and held her hand. With the other she blessed him while I stroked his feet. Mary invited Dad to pray silently with us, to prepare his soul for the presence of God, and to rest in God's grace as he slept. She asked for angels to guard him, for fear of death to diminish, and for new life to surge into him. Dad went to sleep shortly thereafter. I did not see him alive again. I sat next to him until around 9:00 and went up the street to my sister's house for a bite to eat before going to bed myself.

Sixth, I received a call around 3 a.m. that Dad had passed away shortly after 1 a.m. What would I like to do? I said I'd be there in 20 minutes. And so I was. Irish Mary was in the room with Dad waiting for me. I felt a strong presence in the room. Grace? The spirit world? God? All I know is that I felt reverent being there. Mary and I went to Dad's bed, touched him, and prayed again together. Mary told me she had anointed him every hour since I left. The stronger drugs had eased his discomfort immediately, and death had occurred quietly in his sleep. We sat in the room for the next two hours awaiting the black hearse. We sang "Amazing Grace," we read the full version of the 23rd psalm, and we sang other hymns that came to mind. The sacredness of that time was unmistakable and unforgettable. Perhaps Mom had come to bring Dad home. When the hearse arrived, it was a little after 5 a.m. Mary and I helped the funeral director put Dad's body in a bag, and I zipped it up. We took the elevator to the lobby, smelling coffee from the kitchen. I was aware that no one was around. Wouldn't that be Dad's way? He would have hated being the focus of a parade. So, silently, we left the empty lobby that in another hour or two would be filled with residents. God was gracious to him . . . even to the end.

Seventh, my brother Bill, in California, had checked in with my sister mid-afternoon Sunday, and she had relayed dad's status. His intuition told him to do something immediately. He cancelled work and booked a seat on a red-eye to Newark. He was on his way and arrived five hours after dad died. Bill's help in the days to come was invaluable. We needed him with us.

## Points to Ponder

Here the sacred journey faces its powerful end. I have become convinced through our parents' stories that much happens spiritually in preparation for everyone's final step.

I believe that death is sacred because the human being is sacred. If we are blessed to spend this brief period of time with loved ones, life touches us in ways that defy words. If our loved ones are alone when they are passing through this valley of the shadow, perhaps others who have already passed are hovering to welcome them into an eternal home. I've heard many stories about people looking outward, almost beyond the room where they lie, with a smile on their face and a name on their lips. Someone has come; they are not alone.

Many of us notice serendipitous events that miraculously converge in the final days. Perhaps, the several events that occurred on Dad's last days were his miracles.

You might use a different word from "miracle." But this one works for me, because I see a miracle as someone or some thing that appears in one's path in an unforeseen manner, fortuitous and life-altering in a mysterious, holy way. My being in New Jersey that weekend, my sister's request that I stay, the call from the old friend, and Irish Mary' holy water—all fall within that definition.

Many of us fear witnessing the moment of death, feel awkward in these sacred moments of grace, and focus solely on the loss. The loss is real but so is the sacred moment. Consider that more is happening in the last days of life than preparing for death.

Below are four final stories that all relate to families facing the death of a loved one. Each one gives us a different perspective, and one would hope, another opportunity . . .

## Samantha's Change Of Heart

Sam's story is a recent one. This friend and colleague in Virginia is 40; her dad died at age 65. Over lunch one day, she shared her story. Four years ago, Sam's dad—who was, as usual, drunk—made some seriously disparaging remarks to her boyfriend. When Sam and her boyfriend left the house that night, she closed off contact with her father for three years, only reopening the door when her sister reported that he'd been diagnosed with Lou Gehrig's disease (ALS). When, soon thereafter, Sam visited Dad, he opened his arms to her with joy.

Strange as it may seem, the meeting was not an awkward one. Sam knew her dad was very sick and felt sad for him. The rest of her emotions just melted away. She'd heard from her sister that he'd been abnormally tired for the better part of a year, a sign that something was wrong. The disease would claim his life in only fourteen months.

Over time, Sam emerged as her father's primary caregiver. She began to take care of him because she didn't want to feel any lingering guilt; it was the reason she'd agreed to see him again in the first place. Though no one had directly asked her to take the lead in her father's care, she did so, knowing deep down that she was best equipped to handle the many tasks involved. Early on, the care included sharing shifts with her sister and Debbie, her dad's long-time girlfriend. During the last six months, the three women alternated round-the-clock care.

Sam's dad was in a great deal of pain, and toward the end gave up on physical therapy; he also stopped taking his medications. There was some talk about placing him in a nursing home, but everyone knew he didn't want to go, and they were happy to be at his house, in a familiar place. During those months, Sam, her sister, and Debbie would learn a lot about an ALS patient's needs. For one thing, he was on oxygen and the mask kept breaking, which meant that they—mostly Sam—had to drive quite a distance to the only store that kept this equipment in stock. He also needed a flotation mattress and other specialty items. Sam searched the Internet and called all over town and beyond, in search of businesses that sold them. If his ALS medications, which were provided by the Veteran's Affairs office, were not delivered on time, he would go into hysterics. Sam would stay with him, watching him cry like a baby, feeling at a loss for how to console him.

During their time together, her father never mentioned the incident that had broken their relationship. It seems he had no recollection of the event. Sam was skeptical, but she chose not to press him on it.

Sam's father died a little over a year after their reunion. As Sam put it, "Some special things happened to give me peace. That peace is more important to me than anything. I did not love the dad who was well before ALS. I loved the daddy who got sick. That may sound strange. But, last year, daddy said "I love you" to me for the first time since I was a kid. He was nice to me and kind . . . and even though I know he still wanted to drink, except for a few beers, he was never drunk again."

On her dad's birthday, after his death, Sam went to the cemetery and brought a bottle of Busch Beer with her. She poured it over his grave and said, "Happy Birthday, Daddy!" She called Debbie afterward and told her. Debbie laughed and then shared something with Sam that she hadn't known, something that touched her to the core. "Your daddy prayed every day for a miracle," Debbie said, "and I told him, 'you already got your miracle. You have your family back.'"

## Points to Ponder

I am touched by this story because doing the right thing was never the goal for Sam. It's as though she bypassed "doing the right thing" and moved right into forgiveness. Once she opened her heart, the rest followed naturally. How blessed she is to be able to remember her daddy as saying "I love you," rather than remaining stuck on the toll of the disquieting years of his addiction.

In addition, the leadership role requires certain skills. Sam knew she possessed them; she ran her own business, managed her finances, and had lived independently for many years. Without usurping her sister's role, Sam found a way to employ her well-honed skills in a useful manner. Neither her sister nor Debbie objected. With each succeeding task, Sam's suggestions seemed the most practical. Without her having planned to take the lead, the lead became hers to assume.

This type of scenario is not uncommon in families. If all family members allow the natural process of selection to fall into place, conflict is often avoided, and respect is retained. Some people are better leaders than others, yet everyone's role is appreciated.

Lastly, Sam's Busch Beer ritual at the cemetery was tender and important. Dad was probably an alcoholic whose drinking had harmed the family over many years. At the least, it contributed to the demise of his marriage and a rift in his relationship with Sam. Pouring the beer over the grave signified that Sam had made peace with his addiction; it also gave proof of her understanding of the disease. To the end, her father would want to drink beer if he could. It was the nature of the beast. She received her "I love you," and she could, in turn, acknowledge her father's limitations. Such is at the very foundation of peace.

## Deathbed Reconciliation

Dan lived in California with his wife and kids, while his dad, long divorced from Dan's mother, lived in rural Tennessee. He visited his dad once a year, even after Dad went to an assisted living center. Other local relatives tended to him regularly. Dan still harbored the memory of wounds from his father's leather belt, the painful instrument brought out to scare his child into submission. In his adult years, Dan did what he could to respect his dad . . . but in his heart, he had not forgiven him those harsh punishments. Dan called monthly, sent pictures of the kids, and talked on that superficial level that can hide a multitude of needs. When his father came down with a terminal cancer, Dan took a leave of absence, kissed his wife and kids goodbye, and flew to Tennessee to be with him.

Dan never left his father's side. His hungry inner child's heart longed to hear something from him that could redeem the past. He washed his dad's face, rubbed his feet, smiled, and told family stories. One day, toward the end, Dad, who'd heard his own inner noise blasting over the years about how his son had abandoned him, reached beyond that hurt, and said, "I love you, son. Thank you for being here." Dan never did hear "I'm sorry," but his heart softened at those words. He turned to his father and said, "I'm sorry, dad," with tears streaming down his face. He was sorry for having been so stubborn and staying away so long.

He never would hear the exact words he longed to hear. So be it, he thought, as he held his dad's hand at the moment of death. He resolved not to harbor so much resentment toward anyone ever again.

## Points to Ponder

When people hold on to anger or hurt for decades, the emotion takes its toll on other relationships as well. It's as though we demand that another person change, or become what we want them to be, before we can find peace or inner freedom. That we need this is a lie. Freedom is a personal choice, no matter what others do or don't ever do. Sometimes, living a life that reflects that inner peace is compelling and calls others into it too. Candid conversations can clear the air more readily, without demands, guilt, shame, or hate.

I am quite sure that Dan has other therapy work on his plate. When he returns home and reviews his life choices with his wife and children, he may discover ways in which he has affected others with his "inner demand" script. Yet, with the reconciliation he found at his father's side, he has more tools at his disposal to work out whatever may be out of sync with his nuclear family.

## "A Vision of My Mom as God Intended Her to Be"

Gail, a long-time friend, was an only child in a family where the parents divorced early. She was close to her father. She held him in her arms when he died and prayed for him quietly. She had always adored him, even though she was often angry with him for abandoning her mom.

Gail had a different kind of relationship with her mom, who came from an alcoholic home. Her mom carried the classic symptoms of an adult child of an alcoholic, including being dependent on men to take care of her. She was unusually pretty, naïve, sweet, and flirtatious. She was also unfailingly meticulous in her grooming and beautiful to the end. But her mom lacked that certain confidence that most adults develop at some point, a limitation that remained a sore spot with Gail for most of her adult life. Gail would become what therapists label the classic parental child, becoming wiser and more responsible than her mother. In her 80s, Gail's mother met and married a gentleman in his mid 90s. He swept her off her feet. Mom's new husband paid off all her bills and took care of her well. Then her mom contracted an illness from which she would not recover. Gail stayed in touch with her by phone regularly. They had good talks at the end.

One day, while sitting in her living room armchair during her morning prayer time, Gail had an insight—a revelation of sorts. In her heart or her mind's eye, she saw her mom as God intended her to be: a person not compromised by an alcoholic dad or distorted family dynamics; a woman free to be beautiful inside and out; the whole person God meant her to be from the beginning of time.

This insight changed Gail's heart. She could walk with her mother in a new way. She could hear her with a new ear. She could see beyond her mom's characteristics to what was supposed to be and what would be again in the next life. Gail's negative memories dissipated in an instant—she knew only love for her mother. When family would later recall some disquieting incidents, Gail was surprised that she'd forgotten them. Washed away! Clean slate! All Gail saw was the vision of a whole woman who was easy to love.

Her mom began to fail shortly thereafter. Gail flew to her side and was there at the end. She called a friend while sitting by her mother's bed. In a soft, tender voice, she said: "Mom looks so frail. I have no more anger. It's gone. All I have is this tremendous love for her."

Gail had been gifted with a graced awareness of a truth that lies beyond normal vision. Maybe it's there for all of us, if we quiet our beings enough to see it.

## Points to Ponder

Many people are embarrassed to speak from the spiritual plane. Yet it's an essential facet of us all. We may find it in music, art, intimate love, a history book, or alone on a hillside. Whatever our own experience, we'll find our spiritual center if we are open to it because it's there to be found. Some people will live out an expression of this inner capacity through their church, synagogue, temple, or mosque. Others may never step into a spiritual building yet know a presence they call God or some other name.

This spiritual component of our being can remain elusive and private. It is often accessed beyond normal language. Don't let this distract you from its search. Finding our spiritual center completes us as human beings and allows us to love openly, with forgiveness, hope, and joy.

Gail's spiritual experience allowed her to "see" beyond her old experience of her mother. New understanding that ushered in forgiveness erased lingering memories and brought her into communion with her mother's essence. Does such a gift await us when we are open to our own spiritual centers? I'd like to think so.

## Final Recognition: "I Know Who You Are."

Fran is a nurse by training, now retired from her profession. Six years ago, she and her husband took on the care of her mom and dad in the family home. Both parents were quite ill and incapable of self-care. Caregivers were hired for two eight-hour shifts daily. Fran was the night nurse, so to speak. She kept a baby monitor in her room and tended to either parent as the need arose. And a need seemed to arise at least once each night in the early years, more often as they deteriorated physically.

When her dad died two years ago, Fran knew it was time to care for her mom differently. She placed her in a local nursing home, where Fran continued to visit her daily.

Her mom did not grow old well. She demanded a great deal of attention and expected that others would bow to her wishes, no matter how unreasonable. Fran and her mom had already been on different wavelengths for many years, and her mom's decline only polarized them further. Fran worked harder each day to be worthy of some acknowledgment from mom. Thanks and praise never came.

Fran went to the nursing home daily and often brought daisies, her mother's favorite flower. She oversaw medication choices and monitored the staff's follow-through of doctors' orders. No matter how poorly her mom had treated her, Fran's loyalty and dedication to her care prevailed.

Fran's mom had a mini-stroke on a Saturday, and some paralysis ensued. When caring for her, Fran propped her head up to give her a more dignified look. She sat with her in the bed and cuddled her mom under her arm. Drawing on her nursing skills, Fran wanted to see how much her mom could connect with her. So she asked her mother if she wanted water.

What happened next turned a decade of miscommunication into a loving memory. When her mom said, "Yes, please, I'd like some water," Fran was surprised by the gentleness of her mom's response. It was not her mother's usual style. Fran then asked her if she wanted another blanket. She said, "No, thank you." Again, the quality of her voice was completely different from the caustic tones Fran received regularly. What was happening? Fran asked her mom if she knew who she was. "Of course, I know who you are. You are my daughter Fran." And her mom smiled.

Fran was speechless. She hadn't heard her mom speak so sweetly to her since she was a child. No insults, no criticisms, no sarcastic smirks on her face—just gentleness, warmth, and respect. Fran's mother looked her in the eye and moved her hand toward Fran's. Fran went the rest of the way and took her mom's hand into her own. No words about the past were exchanged. No "I'm sorry" or "Please forgive my cutting ways." Just a smile and a "thank you." Something inexplicable, full of grace, had happened to turn a decade of miscommunication into a loving memory.

Unknown to Fran, her husband had come into the room and heard the exchange. He also witnessed the two women reaching their hands out to each other. He captured the moment with his digital camera. Fran intends to frame the picture.

## Points to Ponder

"We never know the day or the hour." This well-known expression about death is often used as a way to prepare ourselves for death, knowing that it can come at any time. I'd like to use this expression now as an indication that we never know the day or the hour when we will be blessed in another's company, as Fran was blessed.

The story speaks for itself. Fran's mom entered the present moment, and it was enough for them both. I wish the same for you in all those significant relationships that go beyond words.

# 11

# The Sum of All Stories
## *Connected Forever*

The stories I've shared all come from real people, mostly in current-day situations, each with their unique growing-older families. I pose the following question for you to ponder in your own family setting: Is aging a family affair for you? For most of us, it is so.

Last week, a close friend's 79-year-old mom had a massive heart attack, sending her beloved family into a tailspin. This week, four funerals were conducted in my church—all for people between 65 and 92. One of the deceased hadn't spoken with her family in over a year—they didn't even know she was ill. Tomorrow, I will see two clients whose parents' aging and related illnesses have limited their independence. My clients struggle with what to do.

One thing is certain for them: Changes lie ahead.

How my clients and their families prepare for and work together, or not, to retain their parents' dignity and respect in the coming years is a question to be addressed in the here and now. How adult children make choices for their self-care, while tending to their aging loved ones, is an equally serious family issue.

Is aging a family affair? A few may say: "No! The discord and emotional distances we experience are too deeply rooted. We will never be able to work together at all." Some will have to ponder carefully before responding. Still, for most, the answer will be yes. The stories that have filled these pages attest to the power of family. No matter how we answer the question, we cannot escape the feelings, memories, longings, and hopes attached to our experience as family. They remain inside us throughout our lifetime.

The aging of America invites us to relate to our elderly in loving and respectful ways, with all subject matters becoming fair game. These must include topics of independence, illness, and death. Open communication can honor everyone; non-communication will often wound and alienate those who are doing their best, either to help or to respond to the help that is being offered to them. All choices have their consequences.

When crisis caught my own family off-guard, we learned on the fly, balancing shock, ignorance of existing elder-care options, and pressure from urgent medical needs to place a parent in the appropriate facility. We needed to talk openly and honestly with each other . . . preferably when we were *not* in crisis. We no longer had that option.

Mom had talked easily with most of us about her physical struggles with cancer and about her sense that death was near. Dad never talked to us—not about how Mom's death might change his life, nor his own needs for extraordinary care when the unexpected happened to them both. Because he kept his own counsel, no matter how hard we tried to engage him, we were forced to go outside the box to relate to Dad.

When this crisis hit, my siblings and I weathered our own personal biases to talk with each other without blame or guilt. Some discussions were problematic and at times irritating, but we stayed the course. To our surprise, we grew in trust of each other's good intentions and found new freedom to accept our differing abilities without judgment, or at least with less judgment. Easy to say— harder to do!

Initiating and sustaining serious family conversations may be awkward for many. Early on, those attempts might even be disastrous (as ours were with Dad). Still, it's critically important to wedge open the door of dialogue, even when emotional or physical distance complicates the process. The time may come when we are delegated to tell Mom and Dad that they can't drive anymore, or that they are messing up their monthly bills and daily pills. How distressing it can be, for them *and* for us, to intervene in their lives, unless we've been attuned to their everyday routines and are respectful of their personal choices. Gaining a parent's trust in preparation for candid conversations is essential. We may first need to visit them more often and observe how they live their lives, or ask them a direct question during a phone call: *How did you spend your day today?* Presence, interest, and respect go a long way.

Some of the families whose stories you've now heard were so communication-challenged that none of the actions suggested above could lead to success without tremendous effort and diligence, if at all. Some were tightly entangled, their members over-involved with each other; others were significantly detached, and as a result under-involved. Several different types of challenges impeded efforts at communication in these troubled families.

Let us review these challenges.

1. Unforgiving memories of unhappy childhoods can bring unresolved, distorted issues into the present crisis. Dina's refusal to take her dad's phone calls, Dick's lingering hurt over his father's criticism, Linda's lack of a defined self pitted against her strong-minded mom's deteriorating condition, and Sally's struggle to please her mom in any way possible: all come to mind.

If disjointed and garbled attempts at resolution over the years have fallen flat, the good intentions behind them are also lost. Hard-to-forget exchanges stay somewhere in our memories and simmer over time, rendering many of us ill at ease with family, even on celebratory occasions. Toss in a family crisis involving Mom or Dad, and unrealistic expectations about "family" are sure to boil over . . . again. Carrying emotional baggage and continuing to hope for closure, we may rush to a dying parent's side with the magical belief that love and forgiveness will pour over us out of a dire circumstance. When the same-old, same-old miscommunication and self-protective devices emerge anyway, the glimmer of hope we harbored sinks.

Aging is a family affair, even when our hurts prohibit us from loving well.

2. Many of us live complex, over-committed lives. When our parents are in need of extra care, we may be too busy to focus on their situation and selfishly turn a blind eye to their growing needs. We may tell friends: "Our parents are healthy. They love their golf, their trips, and dinner parties with their friends. . . . They'll be fine." We need them to be independent because our own busy-ness limits our availability to them. To avoid the inevitable guilt, we give credence to our blind eye. It works for a while. The reality that we may not be among the lucky ones whose parents live to a ripe old age independently eludes us. Great Aunt Jane's Christmas and birthday children are an extreme example of such a situation.

Aging is a family affair, whether or not we acknowledge it.

3. For some of us the thought of losing our parents is so painful that we, too, ignore their frailties. Because of our own fears or unacknowledged insecurity, we need them to stay well . . . forever. So, we discount early signs of physical limitations, reframe them as tiredness, the weather, or someone else's fault . . . and wait. This waiting, however, positions us to have to talk about nursing homes and serious illness from a post-diagnosis or post-accident situation, with a weakened, scared, and overwhelmed parent. Not the best option! What, just a few years earlier, might have been a milder discussion about living arrangements and practical decisions, even about DNR and living trusts, is no longer the least bit easy. Joan and her sisters never saw the Alzheimer's disease coming. So, such discussions weren't even on the back burner, and therefore never happened. Ed's case was different. He braced himself for a challenging discussion with his parents about their aging needs, and during a weekend visit broke through their barrier of silence. Karen, too, broke the silence imposed by a family's rigid rules, by forcing her husband, Phil, to face his parents' inability to continue to live independently. In their case, this was possible only with crisis intervention—but it was done.

These serious, at times disturbing, challenges to good communication in families are understandable. Still, without prior dialogue, when the unexpected happens and we must talk, we will look in vain for a starting point.

It is not unusual for many of us to withdraw and hold back from talking about changes afoot, even if we are not terribly troubled as a family . . . for several significant reasons:

- Conversations about aging, sickness, extended care, and dying are not everyday communiqués. They require time.
- Illness and mental and physical limitations, including diminished mobility, where a surviving spouse will live after their partner dies, are all sensitive topics between parents and adult children, even for those with healthy relationships.
- The authority of our parents declines at a slow pace, if it ever dissipates at all. We are always their children, and they are always our parents, imbued as that term is with our unique, personal meaning.

Some of us escape all the problems mentioned above. We, parents and adult children alike, adapt better than others to what life asks of us. Personal philosophies or a sense of God and a hereafter ground us in a broad connection to all of life. We accept change and receive aging members as they are. We talk about the future as a natural phase of life. We love openly and converse with each other easily and forthrightly. In this environment, our elderly may even initiate the "when I'm gone" talks. When all or even some of this occurs, aging and its natural transitions become a sweet, predictable, and loving family affair. My mother is a prime example of such thinking. Eileen, who climbed into bed with her mom in their last shared moments, and Margaret, who lovingly embraced her ex-husband at the end of his life, are other examples to savor.

I am excited when a parent initiates a family conversation about the future. Victoria is a model for such initiation. She spoke up and pulled her reluctant adult children into a dialogue they would rather not have had, at least, not yet. Victoria boldly addressed her weakening condition from Parkinson's disease with her adult children, changing the near future for them all.

Is aging a family affair?

Whether we are present for each other or not, whether we are free to love one another or are bound up in an unforgiving past, whether we are connected as a family today or remain painfully distant, all of the stories in this book bear witness to this conclusion: aging *is* a family affair.

# 12

# Embracing Our Own Future
## *Questions along Our Sacred Journey*

I am poignantly aware that my own aging story is in the making as I write. Because I live in this era of connection, wide-range information, and a growing number of friends and companions on life's aging journey, I have confidence that I'll be able to live out my later years with thoughtfulness and peace. The stories that have unfolded on these pages are yours and mine, too. They give me hope.

I want to share some of the points that hit home while I was compiling this work. I was deeply touched by my parents' different choices and those of the many people who shared their journeys with me during the last several years. I will be eternally grateful for their candid comments. Their stories have compelled me to prepare more fully for my own future.

Aging is a family affair, whether or not we are intimately connected to our family in their elder years. This I believe more strongly than ever. I hope that these stories will strengthen the decisions you've already made to connect with your family; I hope that they will open new options by piquing your interest.

Seven different aspects of the journey stand out for me. I've articulated them to myself in the form of questions. Perhaps, you, too, may find these questions useful as an outline for your own contemplation:

1. *What is it like to grow older and experience the early signs of aging?* Are we inclined to dismiss these signs, or do we receive them as invitations to prepare for our own aging journeys?

   I often tell people how old I am for shock value. I do not look the way most people think I should look at my age. Yet, I am profoundly aware of new memory challenges, how hard it is to lose weight, unfamiliar aches in my joints and fingers, and the many medications that I take daily. I am aging. I find that such a strange statement because I feel young and alive inside. In my mid 60s, life is great. I'm healthy enough and in a new marriage, of all things. But I realize humbly that the greater part of my time on earth is behind me. To that end, I will do my best to prepare myself and my children for the end time.

2. *What kind of relationships do we have with our children?* Do we want to change anything, tell them anything we haven't already told them?

   I suppose that I'll always want to be "mother" and think my children will continue to benefit from my wisdom until I can no longer speak. My healthier self knows that this is not true. I am impressed with the skills and wisdom demonstrated by both of my daughters with the experiences and challenges that life has put before them. Who am I to tell them how to listen to their own spirit for the rest of the journey? I have enough trouble listening openly to my own. I hope they will take from my choices what is useful to them and be respectful of the rest.

3. *What preparations have we made for our wills, living trusts, and health directives?* Do we know our

children's strengths and limitations such that we can assign them tasks that will bear fruit?

I can only reaffirm the need to accomplish these tasks sooner rather than later. I have completed most of the actions required of me. The rest will be completed before this book is published. That's a promise to myself. It's easy to say "I'll finish the living trust . . . tomorrow." What a shame if someone doesn't have tomorrow. Too many people in my age bracket are dying. You and I may not be among the lucky ones.

4. *Beyond clarifying communication with our loved ones and completing legal and financial business, what else does life ask of us before we die?* What is unfinished in our lives that we must complete, or at least attempt to complete?

I list below those items that are important for my own journey. Perhaps they will give you insight for your own path and call forth some specific actions.

a. I need to organize my office. I don't want my children to have to wade through my stuff to decide what to keep and what to discard. I have a lot of stuff!

b. I need to sift through those items that are important to me, items I want to leave to my children and to other people. I need to write down my choices. I have little treasures I want others to remember me by. The treasures I have kept from others who have gone before me connect me to their spirits. I am just a link in the chain of life, but it has been an honest link, and holding on to other links (through treasures) grounds me.

c. I do not know what is unfinished in my life. I have lived each day to the fullest. I try to listen to God within me for ways to be. To the degree that I have done that well, nothing is unfinished. To the degree that I have been distracted, I pray that my spirit opens to what I've missed and that God allows me to complete my journey.

5. *What do we imitate in the way others have prepared for their later years?* What would we do differently?

a. I want to be open with my family about my faith, my needs, and my feelings— this book is one step toward that endeavor.

b. I want to have all my legal papers in order and talk with my children about them just as my parents did. I want to do this sooner rather than later.

c. I don't want to move in with my children when I am no longer able to live independently. My hope is that my husband and I will live to a ripe old age together, healthy, and happy. Yet, reality invites me to prepare for other options. I want to save my dollars to afford an assisted living situation like Dad's, even if I, too, am there only for six months.

d. If I am required to live in a nursing home for a while, I want to remember the stories I've shared in this book and make the most of that period of time. I want to remember that my children and their children have lives of their own, that they love me and want to honor me, but that I will have alone times for which I must prepare my mind and heart as well.

e. I want all doctors to tell me the hard truths about an illness, and I want my children not to be afraid to talk with me about my end-of-life time. I desire open communication at every stage.

f. If I develop Alzheimer's disease, I want my children to remember my cogent times, work with the setting I'm in for my care, but not to burden themselves with guilt over demands I may put forth, negative feelings I may share, or repetitions I can't stop from making. God may be preparing my tired mind for other things. I trust my family's wisdom to do what they think is right, whatever that may be.

6. *Do we harbor any regrets?*

I harbor a great many regrets for which I ask the forgiveness of those I've harmed along life's way. As I look back, even now, I can see people I did not love well, did not understand well, and did not forgive well. Without the option for another do-over, I am left with the truth in my heart that we will all share in the next stage of life, after death.

I regret my limited ability to love and be loved in my first marriage. I regret the immaturity that guided my early parenting. I regret the massive amounts of female gossip I've participated in over far too many years. And, perhaps like you, I regret other things that are too private and personal to express.

7. *What beliefs (about life, death, God) guide us in the last quarter of our lives?*

a. I believe that all of life is a sacred journey because all human beings are sacred.

b. I believe in a loving God Who called me into being for a limited period of time and allowed me to seek and find love in a great many people. I only pray that I have loved back enough to honor how much I have been given.

c. I believe in a God of Love who will embrace me in enormous Love on another plane—whatever that looks like or feels like. I am sure that it is all at once the essence and the fullness of life's blessed opportunities.

d. I pray that when my time comes my spirit will be ready for the journey through the valley of the shadow into the Light. If I forget, I pray that those around me will remind me.

e. I pray that an "Irish Mary" will be around when I need her to anoint me with holy water and pray me through my final breath.

Such are my thoughts at this stage of my journey. May you open your heart to your own answers to these life questions and, in so doing, find the peace that surpasses understanding.

# 13

# Closing Comment

The final chapter of my mom and dad's story was written a year after Dad's death. When Mom died, we promised Dad that we would not bury her until he could be present.

In the end, we kept our promise. We designed, ordered, and placed the headstone in the cemetery after Dad died. Mom's ashes remained at the funeral home, until we were ready to inter her ashes with Dad's ashes. The one and only gravesite service was conducted in June, 2007, when they were laid to rest together. It was probably what Mom wanted. It was exactly what Dad wanted. It's all we knew he wanted.

Till we meet again . . .

**Mary Ann Massey**
www.AgingIsAFamilyAffair.com

# Notes

# Notes

# Notes

# Notes

# About the Author

Dr. Mary Ann Massey, Ed.D. (www.AgingIsaFamilyAffair.com) has been a licensed Marriage and Family Therapist for over 30 years, working in all settings, counseling families, couples, and individuals regarding a wide range of clinical issues (intimacy, divorce, addictions recovery, stress, depression, intergenerational family relations, aging, personal and spiritual growth, work stress, life transitions, loss, anxiety, and others). She is currently as full-time clinician at The Williamsburg Centre for Therapy in Alexandria, VA. As President of Woman to Woman Live, for almost a decade she has offered an interactive website for women's personal and spiritual growth, providing tele-counseling services (eTherapy), meditations, discussion rooms, counseling column, and articles. She also designs and leads personal growth seminars for women of all ages, as well as seminars on life transitions and aging. Dr. Massey holds an M.S. in Marriage and Family Therapy from Syracuse University and an Ed.D. in Educational Leadership from Florida Atlantic University, Boca Raton, Fla., with additional global training and experience in Zurich, Switzerland (the Jungian Summer Institute) and the Second International Conference on Aging (Amsterdam).

**Tian Dayton, Ph.D.**
**MOTHER MOTHERING**
*How to Teach Kids to Say What They Feel and Feel What They Say*

From her appearance on *Oprah* to her role as a mother, professor, and counselor, Tian Dayton helps us to see the importance of the mother-child relationship. How do children actually learn to articulate their emotional needs? Dr. Dayton offers a remarkable solution, showing how mothers can guide their children to emotional literacy in order to find their true selves, express creativity, and lead productive lives.

978-0-8245-2340-4, paperback

*OF RELATED INTEREST*

**David Code**
**TO RAISE HAPPY KIDS, PUT YOUR MARRIAGE FIRST**

All parents want their children to be happy, but many couples today go too far, letting everything revolve around their kids. This hurts the children and the marriage. The good news is you don't have to choose between your spouse and your kids. Drawing from the latest research in neuroscience and his study of families around the world, David Code offers you practical tools to bring greater simplicity and joy to your family. In this book, you'll learn:

- How confronting your anxiety liberates your children
- Why it's okay to have tough arguments
- How reconnecting with your parents can improve your own parenting
- Why you already have the perfect spouse
- ...And much more.

978-0-8245-2538-5, paperback

Check your local bookstore for availability.
To order directly from the publisher,
please call 1-800-888-4741 for Customer Service
or visit our website at *www.CrossroadPublishing.com*.